Bad Girls and Dirty Picture

Bad Girls and Dirty Pictures

The Challenge to Reclaim Feminism

Edited by
Alison Assiter *and* **Avedon Carol**

Pluto **Press**

LONDON • BOULDER, COLORADO

First published 1993 by Pluto Press
345 Archway Road, London N6 5AA
and 5500 Central Avenue
Boulder, Colorado 80301, USA

British Library Cataloguing in Publication Data
A catalogue record for this book is available from
the British Library
ISBN 0 7453 0523 7 hb
ISBN 0 7453 0524 5 pb

Library of Congress Cataloging in Publication Data
Applied for.

Designed and produced for Pluto Press by
Chase Production Services, Chipping Norton
Typeset from author's disks by
Stanford Desktop Publishing Services, Milton Keynes
Printed in Finland by WSOY

Contents

This book is for
Caroline Norton and Norma McCorvey,
in thanks for
our own money and our own bodies.
And, as always,
for Josy.

Preface

Work on this book began at a time when discussion of the issues addressed herein seemed to be entirely one-sided, and all women were being represented as advocating even more strict censorship of pornography than we have now. This was said to be the 'feminist' position – but not all feminists could agree. It is for this reason that Feminists Against Censorship was founded in the spring of 1989, to provide a voice for the many feminists who could not accept censorship as a useful tool for women. This volume is an offshoot of that effort to re-examine censorship and sexuality from a feminist position.

In the intervening period, things do seem to have changed somewhat. The feminist anti-censorship arguments have begun to filter into the media, and many women's groups have re-evaluated their positions on these issues. At the same time, however, new legislation is being drafted that would make it easier to prosecute an even wider range of sexual materials. The fight isn't over yet, by any means.

As we prepare our final drafts for the material herein, Madonna's book, *Sex*, has hit the shelves and caused quite a stir. Journalists have given interviews themselves to describe the contents of *Sex*, all too often finding it necessary to explain whether or not they personally fancy the author – not something we would expect in the case of a book about sex produced by a man. While some commentators either praise or deplore Madonna as a musician while also deploring the book, most of us have already made up our minds that the music is really beside the point. Madonna is the living symbol of what we already know: that bad girls and good girls are one and the same. Meanwhile, a Conservative MP made a complaint about the book to the Crown Prosecution Service, who, thankfully, decided that we did not need the police to protect us from Madonna.

Under the circumstances, we thought it superfluous to risk prosecution or customs embargoes by printing salacious pictures ourselves. Instead, we have asked anti-censorship women from a variety of backgrounds to give their own views of the sexual battleground. Along with the predictable presence of long-time feminist activists and serious academics, we have included women who feel alienated from the movement and who have not been protected under the stamp of 'respectability' – those who have worked in the sex industry, or in the 'pink collar ghetto' of secretarial and marginal office work, or even as nannies and cleaners. We feel strongly that much criticism of sex work rests in the lack of recognition given to the exploitation of women outside the sex industry who have neither comfortable jobs in the 'alternative' economy nor the freedom of academics and writers who work at home or who have their own secretaries. We can't always agree with each other, but there are many women with different ideas that should be heard and considered. For this reason, we have tried in this book to provide a forum for the women who object to the anti-sex/anti-pornography campaigns and who feel they have too often been denied a chance to represent their own views, as women, in that discourse.

Notes on Contributors

Alison Assiter is a feminist writer and lecturer. For many years, she taught philosophy at Thames Polytechnic, but she has recently moved into managing a programme of developmental projects at North London University, concerned to increase access to employment for 'minority' groups of students. She is the author of *Pornography, Feminism and the Individual* (1989) and *Althusser and Feminism* (1990), both published by Pluto Press. She lives in London and has one son.

Avedon Carol was active in the US civil rights movement and the anti-war movement before devoting her attentions to women's liberation. A former singer and women's health counsellor who also has suffered the indignities of the 'pink collar' ghetto, she is a founding member of Feminists Against Censorship and a current member of the executive committee of the National Council for Civil Liberties (Liberty).

Claudia is the author of *I, Claudia, Love Lies Bleeding*, and other Class Whore Productions.

Alison King is a PhD research student at Reading University. She was the only undergraduate member of the Thompson and Annetts' team which studied British soft-core magazine content in 1990. She is currently researching ritual abuse theories and social worker practice.

Christobel MacKenzie is an anarcha-feminist who has been quietly active for many years in international feminism, and is a member of the Anti-Sexism Campaign.

Tuppy Owens is the publisher of *The (Safer) Sex Maniac's Diary* and other publications, the organizer of the annual Sex Maniac's Ball, and the driving force behind the Outsiders.

Nettie Pollard was an early member of the Gay Liberation Front and a member of the women's liberationist *Red Rag* collective, and has worked for the National Council for Civil Liberties for two decades. She is a founding member of Feminists Against Censorship.

Gayle Rubin is a veteran of the feminist sex wars. She has written many essays on feminist theory, gay history, and sexual politics. She is interested in the process of sexual community formation and is working on a book on the development of the gay male leather community in the United States after the Second World War. She lives in San Francisco with one cat and nine hungry filing cabinets.

Acknowledgements

No book is published without the help of people whose names never appear on the cover or in the contents page, and we'd like to take this opportunity to thank them all. They range from the feminists whose work we found inspiring and thought provoking, whether we agreed with them or not, to the friends, lovers and acquaintances who made interested or supportive comments, put up with our single-mindedness, let us bounce our ideas off them, argued with us. The contributors to this book have expressed disagreement herein with many well-known writers from the feminist movement, but this doesn't mean we don't appreciate the valuable contributions that those authors have made to feminist discourse – without Susan Brownmiller and Andrea Dworkin, we could not always have got as far as we have. From Gloria Steinem to Robin Morgan, Dale Spender to Pat Califia, Susie Bright to Betty Freidan, women all over the feminist spectrum have played their role in helping us shape the questions we ask when we look at the world, and we thank them.

But not, of course, as much as we thank the people who made more direct personal contributions to the work in question: Mog Decarnin, Jane Noll, Roz Kaveney and the elusive Diana, all, in their way, kept the brain cells firing; Suzanna Meredith, Sophie Moorcock, Lulu Belliveau, Joanna, Zak Jane Kier, Elizabeth Coldwell, Isabel Koprowski and Linzi Drew kept us aware that women in the sex industry are not just mindless pawns; Dave Langford and Chris Tame provided technical resources above and beyond the call of duty; Ben Assiter, David Boncey, Vijay Bowen, Whit Diffie, Hazel Farrow, Mary Hayward, Rob Hansen, Val Langmuir, Cyril May, Caroline Mullan, Jo Opie, Deb Percy, Martin Smith, Donya Hazard White, Owen Whiteoak and Anne Wilson contributed more than their share of TLC, coffee-talks, phone calls, drinks, transportation and well-timed smiles in all the right places; and of course, Anne Beech at Pluto provided some much-needed wry humour at important moments. Most of all, we thank our contributors, busy women who squeezed a little more time out of their over-burdened schedules to say what they thought needed saying.

Introduction

'Objective,' as I understand it, means: It doesn't happen to you.
Andrea Dworkin

Women and Feminism

In her discussion of American feminism in *The Dialectic of Sex*,[1]
Shulamith Firestone refers to the public derogation of the suffragist
movement as 'the Fifty-Year Ridicule.' She discusses in some
detail how what Carrie Chapman Catt called '52 years of pauseless
campaign' came to be known, to our own generation, by vague
derisive references to prim little old ladies who, briefly, shook their
umbrellas and squawked for a bit, until the men rolled their eyes
and magnanimously offered female citizens the right to vote.

In the fiery days of the late 1960s and early 1970s when feminist
consciousness overtook the baby boom generation at last, the
knowledge that this was a distorted view of our heritage as women
was just one more source of anger for us. We believed that, with
new technology such as birth control pills and mass communi-
cations at our disposal, we could finally finish the job our
foremothers had not had the resources to complete. This time, we
vowed, men would not stop us.

Today, in the 1990s, we have had cause to recall that the early
historians of this wave of feminism once mourned, those 20-some
years ago, the way the feminist movement of the suffragists had
in many respects self-destructed by splintering off into groups of
those who believed the vote alone would free women, those who
pursued what we would today call 'personal solutions', and those
who had decided that the beastly urges of the male must be
controlled once and for all with social purity movements and
prohibition of alcohol.

Many of us had dismissed those references at the time, believing
that our own generation of feminists could never be led into those
same traps – after all, we had a *radical* approach that took women's
sexual autonomy into account, we knew the biological facts
about sex and gender that had eluded previous generations, we

1

even had the legal right to work and own property, and we were not going to put our eggs into single-issue baskets as our predecessors had done with the vote. Moreover, we were all too well aware that one of the most infuriating sources of oppression and hardship for us was the double standard that had been promoted by the social purity movements, and it was the fight against those very attitudes that was the galvanizing force that made feminism irresistible to many of us. We did not know, then, that the Victoria Woodhulls had been among us all along.[2]

As we have said, the re-emergence of feminism after the Summer of Love made for heady days indeed, with the fresh idealism of our youth and the new liberationist culture, and we believed anything was possible. Internationally, men had been taking off their ties, growing out their hair, and questioning the *male* role, and for women to play our own part in rejecting gender roles seemed a natural course. We were, to say the least, a bit surprised when our male counterparts did not applaud this development.

More than two decades later, our easy dismissal of the shattered feminist movement before the 'fifty-year ridicule' leaves a bitter taste. Leading feminists who had once inspired us now seem to be promoting the same old double standard that had been stunting our lives back in the 1950s. Something called 'cultural feminism' is the fashionable substitute for the sex dualism of our grim and painful youth, and *this*, goddess help us all, is what younger women have been presented with as feminist consciousness.[3]

The new 'feminist' agents of sexual repression have been sullying the reputation of the sexual freedom movement in order to make their point seem more obvious, but their argument – that sexual freedom merely forced women into unwanted sex – is specious. If some men used the rhetoric of liberation as just another 'good line' without understanding it, women only 'fell for it' because we wanted so much to believe it. Sexual autonomy was something that many of us recognized instinctively as much to be desired and in our best interests. Our objection to the awkward and oppressive manifestations of the new culture of sexual liberation should not be mistaken for a wholesale rejection of its ideals (after all, men used feminist rhetoric to pressure women into sex, too, but that didn't mean women's liberation was 'wrong', either); on the contrary, what we found so offensive was that while men were successfully encouraging many of us to shed some of our 'middle-class hang-ups', too many of them were failing to let go of their own. It was not their embrace of sexual liberation, but rather their failure to do so fully, that created the infuriating imbalance between men and women that left us taking all the risks and ultimately holding the bag.

If there was one thing that saved us, it was that sexuality as a whole, both in its more 'respectable' forms and in the vernacular, had entered the public discourse to such an extent that, for the first time in modern history, women had access to its imagery and its language. Although it was largely up to feminists to push the limits of the extent to which we were allowed to use that language, it was the primarily male cadre of anti-censorship activists, pornographers and sexual liberationists who made it possible for us to grab hold of these tools of discourse at all. As people became used to the idea of women participating in that problematic area of discussion, we were more and more often permitted to be true contributors to the lore of sexuality, until we finally realized we needed no one's permission to do so.

Few today seem to remember what it was like 30 to 40 years ago when pornography was often virtually impossible for people to get hold of and sex was never discussed in the company of 'ladies'. Some women today argue the opposing view, that the wider presence of pornography in society has actually reduced the extent to which women are taken seriously in public debate or accorded credibility as authorities in our own fields – yet nothing could be further from the truth.

If women in the 1990s note that men are still given greater stature in public regard, we would do well to remember how much less we had before. In the days when pornography was rare, so were female authorities in the intellectual arena. Even in areas where men could never have any direct experience, they held the credibility of expertise. When it came to knowing what it was like to be pregnant and give birth to a child, or to live as a housewife and mother, or to be a lesbian or a female prostitute, the experts were men – usually doctors, clergymen and psychiatrists. In most cases it would have seemed incredible to consult a woman on the subject of sex – decent women were deemed never to think of the subject at all, and it was considered poor form indeed for a man to bring up such vulgar matters in our presence. The sort of woman who would discuss sex with anyone, or even think of it positively, was a creature too low to be treated with any respect – and who could take the ravings of such a tramp seriously? We were trapped in a catch-22 where we were either too ignorant to know or, if we knew, therefore too disreputable to be given credence.

Thus, men were free to make up their own versions of our experience and feed them to the world. If they were wrong, we were not permitted to say so.

So, in the early days of this wave of feminism, we dissected with some fervour the idea that 'objective' men could have expertise on lives they could not know. It quickly became ludicrous to suggest that heterosexuals could be experts on homosexuals, that men could understand the motivations of female prostitutes, that whites could know the reality of black lives, or that – most preposterous of all – white upper-class and upper-middle-class male doctors had even begun to comprehend female sexuality, let alone acquired expertise on lesbianism. *We* were the experts on female lives, we declared, and *we* would speak for ourselves.

And we were right, of course. Today it is hard to believe, for men seldom dare claim to know more than a woman does about what female life is like. Yet, not so long ago, no woman would dare to describe it, and no man or 'respectable' woman would have listened if she had.

It is only because censorship was reduced and the language of sexuality became a common part of our ordinary lives that we were able to spread the word on sexual issues, publish the insights of our consciousness-raising groups, read women's own descriptions of the parts of our bodies that polite society kept hidden and secret, and begin to understand the extent to which the sex dualism had robbed us.

The men who fought censorship before us did not, in all probability, have women's liberation of any kind in mind, yet we thank them all the same, because they helped to make it seem possible, and that was crucial at the time. It is not they, but others – principally women led by ambitious preachers and politicians – who have tried to remove *Our Bodies, Ourselves*, Judy Grahan's poetry, and *Ms.* Magazine from library shelves in the United States. It is not the men of the sexual revolution, but rather women and men of a latter day, who have sought to push lesbians and gay men back into the closet and women of every stripe back into the bird cage of pallid sexlessness and sacrifice. Whether they are right-wing fundamentalists or political lesbians, they are out there trying to deny once again that women have an authentic sexuality of our own that is a great deal more than the pale imitation of soft-focus romanticism we were raised to believe in.

We have no wish to return to the days where 'good girls don't' and every woman's oppression is reduced to a secret shame. Yet some women who call themselves feminists seem determined to do just that. Today, some of the brightest women we meet, the ones who seem to have the most developed feminist under-standing of sexual issues, are women who refuse to call themselves feminists at all, so loathe are they to be associated with a movement that has become steeped in an ideology of punitive and restrictive attitudes toward women. These are the women who insist on the authority to authenticate themselves, rather than letting others, once again, become the 'experts' on their lives. These are the women who actually argue the issues, who criticize real sexism where it is otherwise accepted, rather than merely using old rhetoric to throw darts at trivial icons.

And these women know that we have let them down. Perhaps this is yet another cycle repeating itself. We look at those old suffragists who lost their fire and allowed the feminist movement to devolve to promoting a sexual purity movement that further stifled women and made feminism look ridiculous – so ridiculous that it would take 50 years for us to revive it once more, this time reacting to the very oppressions those former feminists had left us with. And we wonder if we are now doing the same, if feminism is once again in its dying embers and it is only the dregs we have left.

Those of us who wish to see feminism survive and escape the fate of earlier movements are not prepared to be pulled back into the swamp of sexual repressiveness. Creative women like Della Grace, Rosie Gunn and Naomi Salaman have pursued issues of women as sexual agents despite all proscriptions from left and right, while organizations like the Anti-Sexism Campaign, Feminists Against Censorship, the Lesbian and Gay Freedom Movement, and the S/M Dykes have all tried to re-open the debate and treat sexual freedom, once again, as a vital part of the feminist agenda.

Women and Political Lesbianism

In the 1960s women were trying to pull away from the sex wars of the previous decades and develop a new understanding with men. Because we still believed too much of the ideology of the old sex wars – the stereotypes of women and men – we were ill-equipped to come to any real meeting with men, and we felt betrayed at their unwillingness to participate with us when we finally hit on women's liberation in answer to the questions we were still struggling with.

Women have attempted many strategies to try an end-run around male incomprehension, callousness and sheer pig-headedness. These have ranged from reformist-style attempts to bring women into greater representation in previously male-dominated institutions to a call for 'political lesbianism'.[4] Although some of these designs have been useful in the lives of individual women, the overall structures of the society do not seem to have changed much. Lesbianism, for example, was a hopeful idea for many women, but some found that this was never going to be an answer for them. No analysis of the institution of heterosexuality was sufficient explanation for why individual relationships could not work between women and men, and the vast majority of women still wanted to hold out hopes for what were, after all, their 'first loves' – men. Moreover, accepting that heterosexuality was impossible meant accepting that nothing could be changed, that the whole game was hopeless.

Perhaps more importantly, most women were not interested in a sexuality based on sleeping with one sort of person in reaction *against* another sort of person – that is, using women as a substitute for men. Many lesbians suffered the consequences of heterosexual political lesbianism in which essentially straight women tried to make lesbian relationships that didn't really turn them on, and thus tried to impose their own lack of true interest on their lesbian lovers. No woman wants to believe that someone she loves is with her only because someone else is not eligible or available – being partnered to a straight woman who is really only attracted to men is no less oppressive a prospect than knowing your husband married you in lieu of the 'girl from the wrong side of the tracks' he really loved but his mother didn't approve of. Neither lesbians nor any other feminists were looking to replace heterosexism with nominally lesbian marriages of convenience.

Painfully, lesbian separatists and other politically motivated lesbian feminists made many heterosexual and bi-sexual feminists feel rejected from the movement as a whole.[5] The constant accusation that such women were just giving aid and comfort to the enemy – 'scabbing', as it were – heaped new guilts on these women, taking all the promise out of feminism for them. As the search for female sexual autonomy became eroded under the demand that our desires once again be harnessed to the goals of others, the job of trying to be a feminist came to seem harder and less meaningful than the empty traditional relationships we had left. Indeed, even a number of lesbians felt they were being driven out of their own culture by the intensity of these strict demands for 'politically correct' relationships.

It once seemed a specious evasion to say so, but there is no longer any doubt that political lesbianism is infused to a great extent by an attitude that gives men too much respect, too much power, and too much awe. Some of the best-known thinkers of this part of the movement speak of the male sexual organ as if it held more power than a nuclear device, as if mere proximity to it were enough to ruin a woman forever. This over-emphasis on phallic power seems laughable to any woman who has had close association with the organ in question – after all, we are talking about a few inches of wrinkly flesh here. No matter how much importance some sexist men may accord to the fact that they happen to possess this organ, women, surely, should know better.

Yet the fascinated fear with which political lesbians seem to approach the concept of maleness and the phallus seems to lead them into a circular set of arguments that place all men and most women into categories of tainted disrepute. Both in the US and in Britain, lesbian feminists were still often quite willing to subject bi-sexual and heterosexual women to alienating contempt. In a frightening reversal of institutional heterosexism, some lesbians actually refused to accept a woman's own testimony about her personal experience if she did not reject heterosexuality – thus, lesbians were declaring themselves the true experts on heterosexual lives.[6]

Just as the feminist analysis of the institution of heterosexuality had devolved to condemnation of all individual heterosexual acts or relationships (or people), so had the analysis of transsexualism as a social phenomenon devolved into rejection of individual transsexuals, regardless of their beliefs and behaviour.[7] In some cases we have done serious harm to allies who were never guilty of any behaviour that should anger us.

Feminist fundamentalism and extremism has in fact often stigmatized people and behaviour in this way whenever we have failed to acknowledge and deal intelligently with issues we are unprepared to face up to. We have frequently been guilty of highly destructive – and anti-feminist – acts in the name of the most ludicrously constructed versions of feminist theory. The failure of feminists to come to terms with issues of fantasy and sadomasochism (SM) has thrust whole new levels of guilt on women who have such fantasies or act them out, and the nature of the reaction by anti-SM women can only be termed further oppression of women. Insisting that SM constitutes 'violence against women', anti-SM activists put on ski-masks a few years ago and took crowbars to an SM dyke club, smashing furniture and female bodies as well – this in the name of *protecting* women from violence.

It would seem that feminists have decided it is easier to harass and attack individuals – principally other women – than it is to confront the real institutions of patriarchy. Twenty years ago it would have seemed ludicrous to treat pornography or sado-masochism as anything other than, at worst, mere symptoms of sexist culture, and sheer time-wasting to attack those supposed symptoms while leaving the causal foundations of sexism unremarked. Yet this is exactly what we have been doing. We once criticized the family as fundamental to sexist conditioning, the male role in the family – or lack thereof – as a functional role model of detached uninterest in home life, monogamy as part of a prop-ertarian approach to female sexuality, the culture of romance as an agent of women's oppression. We seem to have forgotten these things altogether, preferring to attack other women for deviating from programmes of dubious value.

Of course, this is a one-sided view of feminism, and one that represents only some groups in a lively and varied feminist culture worldwide. But in the United Kingdom today this is the view of feminism that is most broadly represented both inside the movement and in the general culture.

We have never been able to expect the media to be an under-standing conduit for our best messages, and we are ever being misrepresented as well as co-opted. The fact remains that we have allowed ourselves to be misrepresented even more by our silence when we have allowed small groups of extremists to pretend to speak for all of us. There is virtually no heterosexual feminism of note being represented in this country save for the anti-pornography movement. Feminist programmes with wide appeal seem mysteriously to have slipped into public con-sciousness as either 'Labour Party' issues or as 'lesbian' issues – as if the women's movement had nothing to do with them. Even members of the movement have been guilty of this – books on 'lesbian' issues are published which make only passing reference to interests or experiences which do not hold true for other women, detaching *female* experience from the body of life. Wouldn't it be wiser, and more politically effective, to do the reverse? Twenty years ago, true radical feminists[8] recognized that all women's issues were issues for lesbians, and that lesbianism itself was an issue for all women. From the general image of feminism being presented here today, one would imagine that only lesbians could even care about the most obvious women's issues. Something has gone very wrong, indeed.

Women and the Moral Right

The right-wing moralists have always picked their causes and issues with remarkable precision. If they believe that the availability of pornography is inconsistent with their cause and its goals, we should have no doubt that they are correct. They have opposed every aspect of feminism from the very beginning, in much the same way that they reacted – often with violence – against long hair on men and every other attempt, whether of the most trivial reformism or manifest radicalism, to alter the terrain of sexist oppression. In fact, the reaction against long hair on males in the 1960s should have been recognized as an early warning to us that they are very quick to spot our deviations from their programme, even when we do not.[9] Their vociferous rejection of even the most tepid discussion of sexual issues is wholly consistent with their attitude toward pornography – in both cases, the possibility that people will explore sexuality and learn the truth terrifies them.

It is no accident that the religious right has always embraced censorship, and it is perfectly clear that when their interests and ours appear to coincide, it is we who have to think again about why we have chosen this path – they *are* acting in their own interests, and those are never the interests of feminists.

Although anti-porn feminists continue to deny it, their pro-censorship activities have had increasingly visible support from members of the Christian right. In Indianapolis, local feminists were deliberately kept ignorant of the hearings on pornography, which were set up by right-wing legislators in an attempt to use 'liberal' arguments to promote their own goals. The 'feminist' Dworkin-MacKinnon[10] language may have been used for the purpose, but feminism was the last thing its proposers in Indiana had in mind. Local feminists were furious when they learned – after the fact – about the hearings, and they were vocal in their opposition to the legislation.

In Britain today, conferences and 'debates' held by feminist anti-pornography campaigners are joined by a growing number of Christian rightists who have learned to use feminist rhetoric to their own advantage in this cause. Phrases like 'degrading to women' and 'systematic exploitation' trip so easily off their tongues that you might almost imagine they know and care what those words mean. In fact, many of these people would be happy to see their co-campaigners, quite a few of whom are lesbians, put in jails or worse merely for being who they are. They are 'pro-family' in the most virulently anti-feminist sense, and they care not one little bit about destroying the institutions of patriarchy. They will 'protect' women from any deviation from their prescribed 'Christian' programme, and from nothing else.[11]

Most pernicious among them are those who consistently refer to issues of child abuse in order to make their case. They discuss child pornography as if it were thoroughly legal and easily available, when in fact it is already entirely criminalized and no new legislation could make it more so. They as much as claim that child abuse is largely a function of 'child porn rings' or caused specifically by pornography. This issue is repeatedly raised in order to generate strong emotional reactions, and then a false connection is made with widely available soft-core adult pin-up magazines as if the elimination of the latter would protect children from sexual exploitation.

In fact, the vast majority of child abuse occurs in isolation within the families of men who are not even paedophiles and have no interest whatsoever in child pornography. The common child sexual abuser is a parent, sibling, uncle or family friend who would never think of getting together with others of his kind and chatting about having abused a family member or sharing pictures of similar acts. But, of course, Christian rightists are thoroughly uninterested in pointing a finger at the family as a source of abusive behaviour. It is in their interest to single out 'deviant' groups and practitioners of what they call '60s morality' as the real generators of outrageous acts. Thus, they will promote the popular canard that gay men sexually assault children, when in fact gays are far less likely than 'normal males' to force sex on children. Similarly, they have now latched on to pornography – something else they view as a manifestation of 60s permissiveness – as a cause of child abuse.[12]

There is no reason to take these claims seriously, yet anti-porn feminists and a host of social workers are now accepting and repeating them. Suspicions about such activities are used as pretexts for invading the homes of perfectly well-adjusted, happy children and kidnapping them for traumatic days or months of 'helpful' behaviour designed, it is claimed, to 'protect' kids from adults they love and trust.

In early 1991, on no visible provocation, police and social workers launched a dawn raid into the homes of nine children in the Orkney Islands who were dragged from their beds to be stripped naked before rooms full of adults where they were subjected to intrusive medical examinations by the authorities, against their wills. The children were prevented from taking their teddy bears and separated from their friends and siblings while they waited more than a week for an appeal by their parents to be heard (the parents lost, although their children were ultimately returned to them later).

One must wonder what these authorities were thinking. Whether or not those children had been abused (and there is no reason to think they had been), it should take little imagination on anyone's part to realize that these children were being subjected to something no one should have to go through – wrenched from their homes, separated from those they know and love, made to stand naked before strange adults, asked embarrassing and awkward questions, and kept away from everything familiar to them for an indefinite period of time.

In the same week that the Orkney parents lost their appeal, the parents in another celebrated case in Rochdale were told that there had been 'no case to answer' and had their children returned to them, after many months of separation. These cases result from a growing hysteria over 'Satanic abuse', unproven and clearly the result of religious prejudice and political manipulation, which has been terrorizing otherwise normal households all over the British Isles of late. These outrages are committed in the name of 'protecting children', but one wonders who, at long last, will protect children and families from these terrifying and destructive invasions by police and social workers who apparently care nothing at all for the rights and needs of young people.

Similarly, the children who have befriended paedophiles have also been victimized whenever the police decide it's time to go after 'the perverts'. This can happen regardless of whether the paedophile in question ever makes any kind of sexual overture or contact with the child at all. In many cases the relationship is indistinguishable from the ordinary non-sexual (and often highly beneficial) relationships that many of us have had with adult friends or family members who took an interest in our welfare when we were children. While it is doubtful that they were all paedophiles, it is always possible – although we may never know, as many adults who have no such interests nevertheless lend their aid and comfort in this way to children who are not their own offspring. What is certain is that few of us would have benefited from having those relationships turned sour by a sudden flurry of extreme and frightening activity on the part of police and other strangers who might try to imply that these relationships might or should have been 'dirty' and destructive, when they were not. Adults seem to have little appreciation of the traumatic effect that such interrogations can have on young people. These sleazy affairs never leave a child untouched. If there was abuse, it may be compounded by the 'help' of authorities; if there was no abuse before, there certainly is now.

What is occurring today, in the wake of child abuse hysteria, is that every innocent interaction between adult and child is being called into question in such a way that any human decency an adult shows toward someone else's child can suddenly result in trauma for both participants. Just at the time when some men had started to take feminist demands about child-raising seriously, men are now being placed at a greater distance than ever from children because of a growing paranoia that they can't be trusted around kids.

Before the 'Satanic abuse' frenzy began, day-care centres were the target of these actions in the United States, where the dominant culture of the right persists in pretending that women can not possibly need paying jobs. Day-care centres (and battered women's shelters, which they also object to) pose a real threat to their attempts to keep women chained to the home. It is perhaps no accident, then, that this is where the hysteria first took hold, often giving rise to the theory that no woman could now trust her child for even an hour out of her own sight and that, of course, women should give up their jobs so that they could stay home and protect their kids from all those potential abusers out there. That abuse frequently occurs in the home while the mother is present was, of course, not mentioned.

Child abuse was originally a feminist concern in that we were well aware of how 'experts' in the past spent so much time denying our experience. Many women reported being abused by fathers or other family members, but Freud set the scene in developing the theory that these incidents were nothing more than a phenomenon of female imagination. Rape was often treated similarly and, as both issues dove-tailed with the concept of a woman's authority as the 'expert' on her own life experience, we began to pay more attention to the overt evidence of child abuse and to children's testimony when they seemed to show a decided reluctance for the company of some family members.

The far right were able to prevent the passage in the US of feminist legislation to protect women and children from violence and abuse in the domestic sphere, claiming it would interfere with a husband's rights over his wife and parents' rights over their children, but they suddenly seem to have taken advantage of the anger and fear women have over these issues and turned them into new vehicles for their ages-old programme of repression. We should never for a minute forget how little they cared for the safety of women and children when the issue was addressed in terms of the husbands and parents[13] who were most likely to pose the greatest threat. It is only now, when the targets reside among the least likely sources of abuse, in the margins of society, that the right has jumped on the bandwagon.

Feminists should not be fooled into thinking that a happy accident has brought right-wing interests into line with our own. Instead, the very fact that they appear to be supporting feminist goals should give every woman pause to ask herself whether we have been conned into mistaking their goals for ours. They have never been on our side, and they never will be.

Women and Sex

Females have always been told that our identities reside in our ability to make romantic partnerships, and males have always been told that they must prove their 'virility' by sexual acts with females. But women are *also* told that we are not very sexual and that sexual activity is dangerous to us and 'soils' us – meaning that it is generally in our best interests to foil the attempts of males who wish to act sexually with us. Society also has a way of telling males that loving relationships represent a suppression of their virility, a wife is a 'ball and chain', and that it is women rather than men who benefit from marriage. In other words, we are taught that the needs of women are in direct conflict with the needs of men, and that therefore each encounter between us is a power struggle in which one must lose if the other succeeds. The male wins if he gets sex without the 'responsibilities' of a relationship or marriage; the female wins if she gets the relationship without having to 'sacrifice' sex. Interestingly, the female is never allowed to win permanently in this design – once she has got what she wants (love/marriage), she can 'give in' and allow her husband/lover to have sex with her. If the man 'wins', however, he gets the sex without ever 'giving in' to love or marriage.

This is, of course, a lie. Studies of the the psychological and physical health of married people compared with single people demonstrate repeatedly that men are better off married and women are better off single.[14] Men seem to like marriage just fine once they get into it, and many a married woman has longed to return to her days as a 'single girl'.

But the nastiest part of the lie is the assumption that only men like sex. While it is true that most women's earliest sexual experiences with males would not recommend copulation as an activity, the fact remains that women have sexual feelings, sexual desires, and, ultimately, a lot of us have some very good experiences of heterosexual intercourse. Our perception of sex is no doubt considerably tainted by the fact that our first experiences are with young males who don't know what they want, what they are doing, or even who they are doing it with.[15] Males eventually overcome their need to 'prove' themselves and discover that they, too, have other than sexual interests with their partners – but first they have to struggle with confusing and adversarial situations in which neither they nor the females they are involved with seem to be free of the barriers against honest interactions.

Unfortunately, most of our understanding about sexuality seems to be based on these early adolescent experiences, combined with the 'authoritative data' of marriage counsellors and other sources that examine only situations where the interaction between women and men is problematic or dysfunctional. In other words, we know about relationships that don't work. We have begun to recognize that women seem to enjoy sex a lot more as they get older, but we don't like to spend much time wondering what that means and interviewing 40-year-old women about their sexuality. We like to pretend that it is only the sexuality of *young* women that matters, so we ignore an essential part of our data base – the women who openly enjoy sex.

Of course, we have never wanted to talk much about women liking sex – 'good girls don't', do they? 'Respectable' society silences the 'bad' women, the ones who eagerly indulge in sex, as a matter of course. Many feminists have tended to dismiss positive heterosexual experience as 'myth' or brainwashing. Heterosexual women in the feminist movement perpetually seem to be apologizing for having relationships with men. Lesbians who once tried sex with men who didn't attract them believe their experience duplicates that of straight or bisexual women who 'claim' to enjoy sex with men. Political lesbians who gave up on men long before they ever found heterosexual activity that was to their liking think they, too, know better what those 'straight' women really feel.

But they don't know. The fact is that many women do enjoy sex with men, many lesbians enjoy penetrative sex with each other, and not all heterosexual relationships turn out to be nightmares of sexist oppression. Still, an astonishing number of women simply refuse to believe those other women who say they want sex.

And, refusing to believe, they therefore insist that pornography that shows women enjoying those acts misrepresents women. Whether it is ordinary intercourse, lesbian sex using dildoes, oral sex, or sadomasochism, anti-sex feminists cannot bring themselves to acknowledge that some women make their own choice to participate in these acts because they enjoy them – thus, they say, any film or photograph of such acts can *only* appeal to male sexuality, and the women who pose for such pictures are submitting to having horrible acts committed on them.

Anti-porn feminists also insist that pornography offends women. This statement is a half-truth because, although many women are indeed offended by what they 'know' of pornography, the fact is that a substantial number of women actually enjoy material that is pornography by any definition. Women love to be turned on, and they spend millions on sexual materials: the pornographic video market in the United States is 40 per cent female, the readership of the Scandinavian sex magazine *Cupido* is 40 per cent female, and the readership of *Forum* is 40 per cent female. Soft-core porn – the kind women usually see – has little appeal for most women, concentrating as it does on pictures of women who seem to be mostly inactive and looking for all the world not much different from the women we normally see on TV and in Hollywood films.[16] But women watch hard-core movies and read romance novels that skate perilously close to SM ('bodice rippers'). Women comprise a substantial part of the market for SM fantasy novels in which whole planets of dominant males subjugate submissive females (the Gor series by John Norman, or Sharon Green's SM-oriented MIDA and Terrillian books); in fact, many book dealers insist that *most* of the buyers of these novels are women.

A common piece of rhetoric from the Campaign Against Pornography & Censorship (CPC)[17] and from Campaign Against Pornography is that 'Pornography contains one message', and this is one of male violence and dominance toward women. The hard core men see, however, principally shows equal relationships in which no one particularly dominates anyone, and the SM porn magazines show a far higher proportion of stories in which females are dominant. Given the number of porn films and magazines in which men perform as objects, or as virtual sexual slaves to women, it is hard to believe anyone could get the message of male dominance from modern porn.[18]

Yet both male and female anti-porn activists persist in saying that pornography is a genre aimed entirely at males and carries the messages of female victimization – 'an invitation to rape'. Male members of CPC repeatedly state that looking at pornography caused them to have unpleasant thoughts about women; women who 'testify' against pornography maintain that they learned from looking at *Playboy* and *Penthouse* that the relationship between men and women is one of violence (as in the Minneapolis hearings on the Dworkin-MacKinnon anti-pornography legislation).[19] These are curious claims, since most pornographic media – and certainly *Playboy* and *Penthouse* – show no violence whatsoever against women, and the messages from hard core in general about the positions of males and females are at the very least strongly mixed.

Given this wide disparity between the actual content of pornography and the claims about pornography, we have to wonder just what *is* so threatening about sexually explicit media. And it is not hard to conclude, after looking at the reality of the situation, that the real threat is in subverting the myth that women are largely asexual creatures who dislike sex. Some men are doubtless equally threatened by the idea that sexual desire is not a male preserve – not, then, the 'proof' of virility. Some women, too, seem to be frightened to give up the idea that women are somehow more 'pure' then men, and therefore deserving of the restrictions of the pedestal.

Anti-porn feminists take comfort from the image of woman as the perfect victim in sex – always raped, never thrilled in the arms of a lover. If we admit to taking pleasure from sexuality expressed outside of a 'loving, equal relationship' or in unconventional acts, we are perceived to be somehow legitimizing male violence, rather than acting assertively. Sex for pleasure is treated as a male vice, and women who like sex are written off as being 'male-identified' – that is, we are presumed to be expressing *their* sexuality rather than our own. In either case, the sexually expressive woman is always seen as the victim of male propaganda and male violence. Pornography – the image of women enjoying sex – is seen as the purveyor of this message.

The truth is that pornography contains many messages – messages which are in direct conflict with each other unless it is understood that human beings are many and varied and our fantasies are not necessarily consistent with a single stereotype of male and female roles. Both the moral right and anti-porn feminists are threatened by such messages and seek to suppress them. The traditional stereotype of women has always forbidden us pleasure for its own sake. We are meant only to find fulfilment in serving the needs of others; in the case of sex, we may do it in order to procreate, to satisfy our partners, or to serve societal and political ends. To seek our own pleasure is to commit that greatest of female sins: 'selfishness'.

The threat of being called 'selfish' has always been one of the highest barriers for women – against pursuing careers, making time for ourselves, making relationships with the partners of our choice, or leaving abusive partners. We were raised to feel that we could never choose anything for ourselves, that we must always consider our parents, society, our current or even future mates, and of course the children, before we could make any move. We were often taught to be suspicious of any decisions – even when they obviously would benefit others – if we were also able to obtain pleasure from them. Today, women who wish to pursue their own sexual enjoyment are being threatened with the accusation of 'selfishness' because this, too, undermines the belief that women exist to serve the needs of society, partners, 'sisters' and children, but never ourselves.

Despite these pressures from both the right and the left, from the traditional moralists and the feminist fundamentalists, women have continued to fight for freedom of sexual investigation and expression. Whether we call ourselves feminists, lesbians, straight, bisexual, or just women, we know that we need no more closets to hide what we really are, no more 'experts' to deny our experience to us, and no more loveless lies. We would love our sisters and brothers both, if they will have us – but whether they will or not, we will first know and love ourselves.

1

Misguided, Dangerous and Wrong: an Analysis of Anti-pornography Politics

GAYLE RUBIN

This essay is a revision of an essay based on remarks that were originally submitted as testimony to hearings on pornography held by the National Organization for Women (NOW) in San Francisco, California, on 26 March 1986. Shortly after the hearings, I sent a written version to NOW for inclusion in a collection of bound photocopies of statements on pornography which were made available from the national NOW office. I have kept revisions for this 1992 publication as minimal as possible, but I have made changes to render the piece more intelligible to a contemporary audience and to readers who may be unfamiliar with many details of US politics. I have also added references; some are more recent than the text and consequently induce unavoidable but vertiginous moments of anachronism.

Much has occurred since 1986 and it is impossible to update and recontextualize the article completely without major surgery. So I leave it as something out of time, a period piece unfortunately more prophetic than I knew.

I 'The Empress Has No Clothes'

The targeting of pornography as a focus of feminist rage and political effort has been a dangerous, costly and tragic mistake. Feminists should be aware of the potentially disastrous consequences of this misguided crusade. It is important for feminists to realize that the arguments against pornography are incredibly flimsy, and that there is little intellectual justification for a feminist anti-porn position.

Anti-pornography politics surfaced as a volatile flashpoint in the women's movement in the United States in the late 1970s.[1] Although criticisms of pornography had previously occurred in feminist writing, pornography did not become a major focus of feminist agitation until after the emergence of a group in the San Francisco Bay area in 1976 called Women Against Violence in Pornography and Media (WAVPM). In 1978, WAVPM held a 'Feminist Perspectives on Pornography Conference' in San

18

Francisco. This gathering quickly sparked the formation of New York City's Women Against Pornography (WAP), and marked the eruption of pornography as a popular feminist issue.[2]

By 1978 feminists had already spent a decade identifying and criticizing the ideologies that justified male supremacy and that permeated virtually all of western literature, high art, popular media, religion and education. Ideas of male dominance were deeply embedded in children's reading material, in medicine and psychiatry, and in all the academic disciplines. Similar attitudes were endemic to advertising, television, movies and fiction. Feminists denounced cultural expressions of male supremacy and began to produce new art, fiction, children's literature, film and academic work with different values. Feminists demanded changes in medical and psychological practice and in popular media such as advertising, television and film.[3]

In all of these areas, feminists attempted to reform existing practice and to agitate for non-sexist attitudes. In no case did feminists call for the abolition of the area or domain in question. There were never groups called Women Against Film, Women Against Television, or Women Against the Novel, even though most film, television and fiction were demonstrably sexist. When pornography became an issue, it was treated in an entirely unique fashion. Instead of criticizing the sexist content of sexually explicit media, and calling for the production of non-sexist, pro-feminist, or woman-oriented sexual materials, feminists concerned with porn simply demanded that it be eliminated altogether.[4] Unlike any other category of media or representation, pornography was treated as beyond feminist salvage. The singularity of this position and its underlying premises have too often been overlooked.

Advocates of the anti-porn position commonly declared it to be self-evident and undebatable.[5] They insisted that opposition to pornography was essential to feminism and that by definition a feminist could not dispute the anti-porn position. Those of us who did disagree were dismissed as feminists or smeared with accusations of promoting violence against women.[6]

With little debate, anti-porn ideas became a coercive dogma and a premature orthodoxy. Ungrounded and often outlandish assertions became unquestioned assumptions. Important distinctions, such as those between sex and violence, image and act, harmless fantasy and criminal assault, the sexually explicit and the explicitly violent, were hopelessly blurred. The words 'violence' and 'pornography' began to be used interchangeably, as though they were synonymous. Pornography was often simply equated with violence. This muddled terminology and its conceptual confusions became widespread in the feminist media. Even women who had reservations about the anti-porn position or its consequences often expressed these within the terms set by the language of anti-porn proponents.[7]

It is well known to students of rhetoric that people may become convinced of a false premise or an illogical conclusion if it is merely asserted loudly enough, often enough, or with sufficient conviction. This has occurred in the porn 'debates'. A common tactic of demagogues is to use inflammatory images to drive people into fear and hate beyond the reach of rational discussion. This has occurred in the porn 'debates'. When any discourse is polarized, those not directly involved in the conflict tend to assume that the truth of the matter lies in the middle between the extremes of opinion expressed. This is a dangerous tendency that has often resulted in giving more credibility to the messages of hate-mongering groups than they deserve.[8] This too has occurred in the porn 'debates'.

Many feminists have accepted the notions that pornography is an especially odious expression of male supremacy, that pornography is violent, or that pornography is synonymous with violent media. They disagree merely about what should be done about it. For example, there are many feminists who think of porn as disgusting sexist propaganda, but who nevertheless are concerned about defending the First Amendment and who are cautious about invoking censorship. I certainly agree that concerns over censorship and freedom of expression are valid and vital. However, my purpose here is not to argue that pornography is anti-woman speech which unfortunately deserves constitutional protection. My goal is to challenge the assumptions that pornography is, *per se*, particularly sexist, especially violent or implicated in violence, or intrinsically antithetical to the interests of women.

The 'pornography problem' is a false problem, at least as it is generally posed. There are legitimate feminist concerns with regard to sexually explicit media and the conditions under which it is produced. However, these are not the concerns that have dominated the feminist anti-porn politics. Instead, pornography has become an easy, convenient, pliant and overdetermined scapegoat for problems for which it is not responsible. To support this contention I will examine the fundamental propositions and structure of anti-porn argument.

II Premises, Presuppositions and Definitions

The Conflation of Pornography and Violence

One of the most basic claims of the anti-porn position is that pornography is violent and promotes violence against women.[9] Two assertions are implicit or explicit to this claim. One is that pornography is characteristically violent and/or sexist in what it depicts, and the other is that pornography is more violent and/or sexist in content than other media. Both of these propositions are false.

Very little pornography actually depicts violent acts. Pornography does depict some form of sexual activity, and these sexual activities vary widely. The most common behaviour featured in porn is ordinary heterosexual intercourse (although it is a convention of porn movies that male orgasm must be visible to the viewer, so ejaculation in porn films generally takes place outside the body). Nudity, genital close-ups and oral sex are also prevalent. Anal sex is far less common, but some magazines and films specialize in depicting it. While some films and magazines attempt to have 'something for everyone', a lot of porn is fairly specialized and many porn shops group their material according to the primary activity it contains. Thus, there are often separate sections featuring oral sex, anal sex or gay male sex.

There is also 'lesbian' material designed to appeal to heterosexual men rather than to lesbians. Until the last decade there was very little porn produced by or actually intended for lesbian viewers. This has been changing with the advent of some small circulation, low-budget sex magazines produced by and for lesbians. Ironically, this nascent lesbian porn is endangered by both right-wing and feminist anti-porn activity.[10]

There are several sub-genres of porn designed to cater to minority sexual populations. The most successful example of this is gay male porn. There are many specialized shops serving the gay male market. Much male homosexual pornography is produced by and for gay men, and its quality is relatively high. Transsexual porn is more rare and found in fewer shops. It is designed to appeal to transsexuals and those who find them erotic. Many of the models seem to be transsexuals who are working in the sex industry either because discrimination against them makes employment elsewhere difficult, or in order to raise money for sex change treatment.

Another specialized subgenre is SM porn. SM materials have been used as the primary 'evidence' for the alleged violence of porn as a whole. SM materials are only a small percentage of commercial porn and they are hardly representative. They appeal primarily to a distinct minority and they are not as readily available as other materials. For example, in San Francisco only two of the dozen or so adult theatres of the late 1970s and early 1980s regularly showed bondage or SM movies. These two theatres, however, have always been prominently featured in local anti-porn invective.[11]

Many of the local porn shops have small sections of bondage material, but only a couple have extensive collections and are therefore favoured by connoisseurs. Mainstream porn magazines such as *Playboy* and *Penthouse* rarely contain bondage or SM photographs. When they do, however, these again are emphasized in anti-porn arguments. Some bondage photos in the December 1984 *Penthouse* are a case in point. They have often been used as examples in slide shows and displays by anti-porn activists, who invariably neglect to mention that the occurrence of such spreads in *Penthouse* is exceedingly unusual and quite unrepresentative.[12]

SM materials are aimed at an audience that understands a set of conventions for interpreting them. Sadomasochism is not a form of violence, but is rather a type of ritual and contractual sex play whose aficionados go to great lengths in order to do it and to ensure the safety and enjoyment of one another. SM fantasy does involve images of coercion and sexual activities that may appear violent to outsiders. SM erotic materials can be shocking to those unfamiliar with the highly negotiated nature of most SM encounters. This is compounded by the unfortunate fact that most commercial SM porn is produced by people who are not practising sadomasochists and whose understanding of SM is not unlike that of the anti-porn feminists. Thus commercial SM porn often reflects the prejudices of its producers rather than common SM practice.[13]

Torn out of context, SM material is upsetting to unprepared audiences and this shock value has been mercilessly exploited in anti-porn presentations. SM porn is itself misrepresented, its relationship to SM activity is distorted, and it is treated as though it is representative of porn as a whole.

Pioneered by WAVPM and adopted by WAP, slide shows have been a basic organizing tool of anti-porn groups. Slides of images are used to persuade audiences of the alleged violence of pornography. The anti-porn movie *Not a Love Story* follows a format similar to the slide shows and utilizes many of the same techniques.[14] The slide shows and the movie always display a completely unrepresentative sample of pornography in order to 'demonstrate' its ostensible violence. SM imagery occupies a much greater space in the slide shows and in *Not a Love Story* than it does in actual adult bookstores or theatres.

In addition to SM materials, the presentations utilize images from porn that are violent or distasteful, but that are again unrepresentative. An example of this is the notorious *Hustler* cover showing a woman being fed into a meat grinder. This image is upsetting and distasteful, but it is not even legally obscene. It is also unusual. *Hustler* is a magazine that strives to be in bad taste. It is as different from other comparable mass-circulation sex magazines as the *National Lampoon* is from *Esquire* or *Harpers*.

Arguing from bad examples is effective but irresponsible. It is the classic method for promulgating negative stereotypes and is one of the favoured rhetorical tactics for selling various forms of racism, bigotry, hatred and xenophobia. It is always possible to find bad examples – of, for example, women, gay people, transsexuals, blacks, Jews, Italians, Irish, immigrants, the poor – and to use them to construct malicious descriptions to attack or delegitimize an entire group of people or an area of activity.

For example, in the 1950s, homosexuals were commonly perceived as a criminal population, not just in the sense that homosexual activity was illegal but also in the sense that homosexuals were thought to be disproportionately prone to engage in criminal behaviour in addition to (criminal) homosexual acts. This stereotype has been revived by Paul Cameron, one of the United States' most virulent anti-gay ideologues, whose Institute for the Scientific Investigation of Sexuality (ISIS) publishes vitriolic anti-gay pamphlets.[15]

One of his most extraordinary pamphlets is *Murder, Violence, and Homosexuality*, in which Cameron argues that homosexuality is linked to a disposition for serial violent crime. He claims that 'You are *15 times* more apt to be killed by a gay than a heterosexual during a sexual murder spree' (emphasis Cameron's) and that 'most victims of sex murderers died at the hands of gays'. Cameron employs a great deal of imaginative licence and creative interpretation to make his case. He also uses the undeniable existence of homosexual murderers to jump to the absurd, malicious and unsustainable conclusion that there is an 'association between brutal murder and homosexual habits'.[16]

A great deal of anti-porn analysis is argued in a similar format. It jumps from examples of undeniably loathsome porn to unwarranted assertions about pornography as a whole. It is politically reprehensible and intellectually embarrassing to target pornography on the basis of inflammatory examples and manipulative rhetoric.

Is pornography any more violent than other mass media? While there are no reliable comparative studies on this point, I would argue that there are fewer images or descriptions of violence in pornography, taken as a whole, than in mainstream movies, television or fiction. Our media are all extremely violent, and it is also true that their depictions of violence against women are often both sexualized and gender specific. An evening in front of the television is likely to result in viewing multiple fatal automobile accidents, shootings, fistfights, rapes and situations in which women are threatened by a variety of creepy villains. Prostitutes and sex workers are invariably victims of violence in police and detective shows where they are killed off with relentless abandon. There are dozens of slasher movies characterized by hideous and graphic violence, disproportionately directed at women.

While much of this media is sexualized, very little is sexually explicit and consequently all of it would be completely unaffected by any new legal measures against pornography. If the problem is violence, why single out sexually explicit media? What is the justification for creating social movements and legal tools aimed at media that are sexually explicit rather than at media that are explicitly violent?

In addition, in their efforts to condemn pornography, anti-porn presentations such as the slide shows and *Not A Love Story* often include non-sexually explicit images such as record album covers and high fashion ads. The justification for including non-pornographic images in anti-porn presentations is not always clear. Sometimes it is implied or stated that these images display a 'pornographic' attitude toward women. While it is true that some of the conventional imagery of porn has become more common in the mass media, it is absurd to blame pornography for the sexism or violence of advertising and other forms of popular media.

There is an implicit theory of causality in anti-porn analysis in which a wildly exaggerated role is attributed to pornography in the creation, maintenance and representation of women's subordination. Gender inequality and contemptuous attitudes toward women are endemic to this society and are consequently reflected in virtually all our media, including advertising and pornography. They do not originate in pornography and migrate from there into the rest of popular culture. It is important to recall that rape, violence against women, oppression and exploitation of women, and the attitudes that encouraged and justified these activities, have been present throughout most of human history and predate the emergence of commercial erotica by several millennia.

The inclusion of non-pornographic imagery in the anti-porn slide shows is also justified simply by redefining them as pornography or pornographic. This raises the issue of the inconsistent ways in which pornography is defined throughout the anti-porn discourse.

Definitions: What is Pornography?

The issue of definition – what is pornography and who defines it – haunts the entire discussion and is rarely addressed. This is especially interesting since the definitions of pornography employed within anti-porn rhetoric are circular, vague, arbitrary and inconsistent.

It is difficult to arrive at a precise definition of pornography but at least the complexities can be better situated. According to the *American Heritage Dictionary of the English Language* (1973), pornography is 'Written, graphic, or other forms of communication intended to excite lascivious feelings'. The term 'pornography' was adopted in the middle of the nineteenth century to categorize rediscovered sexually explicit artifacts from the Graeco-Roman world.[17] In the late nineteenth century, sexually frank books and graphic art were rare, expensive and accessible primarily to wealthy and educated men. Although the term 'pornography' was originally used to refer to all kinds of explicitly sexual writing and art, it has increasingly been associated with the phenomenon of inexpensive commercial erotica. Particularly since World War Two, the term has acquired connotations of the 'cheap stuff': mass-market, commercial materials distinct from more expensive, artistic or sophisticated 'erotica'.

According to the same dictionary, erotica is 'Literature or art concerning or intended to arouse sexual desire'. Erotica has had the connotations of being softer, classier, better produced, less blatant, and often less bluntly explicit than pornography.

Neither erotica nor pornography is illegal *per se*. 'Obscenity' is the category of legally restricted sexual speech or imagery. It is important to note that pornography has not until recently been a legal category in the United States. For over a century, sexually explicit materials were illegal only if they were found to be obscene. Although the criteria for obscenity have shifted over time, they have had specific legal parameters. 'Pornographic' was a term of judgement but not of law.

This has now begun to shift and a new category of illegal sexual material that is 'pornographic' but not necessarily 'obscene' is evolving. For example, 'child pornography' is now a well-established legal category in the United States, and the criteria for conviction are broader and less stringent than in obscenity cases. The anti-porn ordinance authored by Catharine MacKinnon and Andrea Dworkin and passed in Indianapolis, Indiana, was an attempt, among other things, to create a new legal category of 'pornography' distinct from 'obscenity'. This new category of 'pornography' would have codified a feminist anti-porn description into law.

Both right-wingers and anti-porn feminists have at times favoured this 'pornography' strategy as a means to circumvent those court decisions on obscenity which have resulted in greater legal protection for some types of sexually explicit material. However, since the Indianapolis ordinance was declared unconstitutional by the United States Supreme Court, subsequent efforts to make pornography a cause of civil action have relied on traditional legal categories of obscenity rather than on the so-called 'feminist' definition.[18]

Within feminism, the debates on pornography have hinged on the definition of pornography. More crucially, the definition of pornography has often functioned as a substitute for argument or proof in anti-porn analysis. Feminists have approached other media with the intention of changing them for the better rather than striving to eliminate them altogether. What distinguishes pornography from other media is the level of sexual explicitness, not the quantity of violence in its imagery or the quality of its political consciousness. Why, then, has pornography alone been considered beyond feminist redemption, and its eradication posited as a condition for female freedom? This breathtaking leap of logic has been accomplished simply by redefining pornography so that it is sexist and violent *by definition*.

For example, in *Take Back the Night* the following definitions are found: 'Pornography, then, is verbal or pictorial material which represents or describes sexual behaviour that is degrading or abusive to one or more of the participants in such a way as to endorse the degradation ... it is material that explicitly represents or describes degrading and abusive sexual behaviour so as to endorse and/or recommend the behaviour as described ... What is wrong with pornography, then, is its degrading and dehumanizing portrayal of women (and not its sexual content). Pornography, *by its very nature*, requires that women be subordinate to men and mere instruments for the fulfilment of male fantasies [my emphasis].'[19] This is argument by tautology. If pornography is defined simply as that which is inherently degrading to women, then by definition it cannot be reformed and must be extirpated. This tactic completely finesses the necessity of providing some demonstration that what is generally thought of as pornography is accurately denoted by such a definition.

A similar definition is at the heart of MacKinnon and Dworkin's so called 'civil rights anti-pornography ordinance'.[20] Catharine MacKinnon has argued that her proposed civil rights ordinance does not hinge on the prevalence of violent imagery within pornography. She has stated that the way a legal definition works is that whatever it would define as pornography would be pornography, so that her ordinance would simply cover whatever fits its definition.[21] This is true, but again the reasoning is circular. It begs the question of why such an ordinance *should* cover pornography, however defined, whether such a definition has any relation to pornography in the usual sense, and why any feminist-supported law should single out sexually explicit materials in the first place.

Moreover, the various definitions of porn employed in anti-porn discourse are not consistently applied. When the targets of anti-porn agitation are identified they are the things more commonly associated with the term 'pornography', i.e. X-rated videos and films, *Playboy* and *Penthouse*, the magazines sold in adult bookstores, lesbian sex magazines, gay male one-handed reading – in short, smut in the more usual sense. If pornography is that which is violent and/or intrinsically degrading to women in one sentence, it cannot be sexually explicit popular media in the next, unless an argument is made that sexually explicit popular media is indeed distinctively violent and/or intrinsically and differentially degrading to women.

Furthermore, the category of 'pornography' seems conveniently expandable. As mentioned above, ads and other media images that are sexually suggestive or particularly sexist are routinely included and called pornographic. Sometimes even sex toys are incorporated into the category. For example, in one of the opening sequences of *Not a Love Story*, as the narrator is describing the ostensible growth and size of the porn industry, the image on the screen shows the crafting of leather wristbands and collars. Whatever one thinks of such items, they are articles of dress and display, not media. In a non-feminist context, the Meese Commission on Pornography has discussed laws prohibiting the sale of sex toys such as vibrators and dildos.[22]

Since few feminists would support the suppression of all sexually explicit media, many anti-porn statements include a disclaimer that not all sexually explicit material is pornography. The residual category is 'erotica'. A distinction is made between 'pornography' (the objectionable stuff against which feminists ought to fight) and 'erotica' (the remaining sexual stuff of which feminists could approve). However, the problems with this approach become apparent as soon as anyone tries to define just exactly what separates erotica from pornography. Early in this debate, Ellen Willis noted with her customary dry wit that most attempts to define erotica and pornography amount to a statement of 'what I like is erotica, and what you like is pornographic'.[23]

For example, the cover of the November, 1978 *Ms.* magazine inquires, 'Erotica and Pornography: Do You Know the Difference?' Inside, Gloria Steinem purports to detail the 'clear and present difference.' Erotica, she tells us, 'is rooted in eros or passionate love, and thus in the idea of positive choice, free will, the yearning for a particular person,' whereas in pornography 'the subject is not love at all, but domination and violence against women.'[24]

In July of 1979 WAVPM's *Newspage* grappled the issue. Acknowledging that 'the question of the differences between erotica and pornography cannot be totally resolved', *Newspage* published a list of distinctions. Among other things, erotica is characterized by this list: personal, emotional, has lightness, refreshing, rejuvenating, creative, natural, fulfilling, circular, and 'just there'. Pornography's list includes: defined by penis, for male titillation, having power imbalance, producing violence, suggesting violence, unreal, elements of fear, mindlessness, heavy, contorted bodies, voyeuristic, linear, and 'something you buy and sell'. Admittedly these lists were summaries of a discussion and not intended as a coherent final statement. But no one has ever been able to come up with a more definitive delineation. These lists are revealing of the arbitrary quality of the distinction. Indeed, one of the few points upon which both Andrea Dworkin and I agree is that the distinction between pornography and erotica is not a useful one for these discussions.[25]

Some anti-porn groups have also exempted sex education materials from condemnation. However, Dworkin has been quoted as wondering 'whether some of the films made specifically for educational purposes contained material as offensive as that found in commercial porn'.[26] In fact, many of the sex education movies are made by heterosexual men whose attitudes toward women are similar to the heterosexual men who dominate the production of commercial porn. This does not mean they all promote violence; it does mean that few of them are paragons of feminist consciousness. To me, these similarities suggest that we should encourage more women to enter both fields as producers, writers and directors. To some anti-porn activists, however, these similarities will be an excuse to include sex education films in their general condemnation of pornography and to subject them to whatever legal penalties and liabilities result from anti-porn campaigns.

Most of the prominent spokespeople for the anti-porn position have also stated publicly that the lesbian sex magazines, such as *On Our Backs*, *Bad Attitude* and *Outrageous Women*, fit their definitions of pornography (indeed, I have heard some of them describe these magazines as 'heterosexual'). Since many of these anti-porn individuals support the passage of legislation to make pornography a cause of civil action, one may infer that they would support bringing civil suits against these magazines.

Despite constant assertions about how porn is 'big business', most of the really interesting porn and all of these lesbian publications are small, low-budget affairs. While *Playboy* and *Penthouse* could survive repeated lawsuits, legal action would put the lesbian sex magazines out of business. Who is going to decide what is 'pornographic', what forms lesbian sexuality must take, and what a lesbian may be able to choose to read? If 'erotica' cannot be agreed upon, if sex education films fit the definitions of 'pornography', and if indigenous lesbian sex magazines are 'heterosexual pornography', what sexual imagery is sufficiently 'non-pornographic' to be acceptable to feminists and exempt from legal harassment?

III The 'Harm' of Porn: Allegations, Assertions and Creative Causality

The Research

Supporters of anti-porn politics have argued that recent research in experimental psychology proves that pornography causes violence against women. The research does nothing of the sort.[27] There are many methodological cautions associated with the kind of research on which the anti-porn position is based. Those studies of pornography show *at most* some changes in attitudes in artificial settings which may or may not have implications for behaviour in real-life situations. The classic experiments, such as those of Edward Donnerstein, used materials that were both sexually explicit and violent, but which were not at all representative of most commercial pornography. At most, the conclusions of such studies pertain only to such materials and cannot be applied to pornography as a whole.[28]

Virtually all the recent studies have exonerated non-violent porn, with the exception of those conducted by Dolf Zillman and Jennings Bryant. However, among the negative effects attributed to porn by Zillman and Bryant are less belief in marriage, greater dissatisfaction with one's present sex life, and greater tolerance for homosexuality and sexual variety.[29] If these are legitimate reasons for condemnation, then feminism and feminist literature are also culpable.

In studies in which subjects appeared more willing to express hostile behaviour after exposure to violent sexual materials, they were asked to decide whether to shock or not to shock a 'victim' after viewing the materials. They were given no other option. For example, they could not choose to be alone, do nothing, or masturbate. In real-life situations, pornography is most frequently used for masturbation or as a prelude to sexual activity with a partner. It would be revealing to compare how many experimental subjects would choose to shock someone if they were allowed masturbation as an alternative.

Finally, none of the published studies thus far have compared levels of aggression after viewing violent sexual material with those after viewing violent non-sexual material. However, Donnerstein is reported to be working on a new study in which it has been found that images of women being beaten but which contain *no* sexual content elicit higher levels of aggression in experimental subjects than images of sexual violence. Donnerstein has publicly cautioned against over-interpretation of his earlier findings, spoken against censorship, and has stated that it is probably violence in media rather than sex which has a negative impact.[30]

The available data are, at the present time, inconclusive, and certainly do not constitute anything resembling proof of broad assertions about the alleged responsibility of pornography in causing violence against women.[31] There is substantial evidence that violence in media is a problem. While there would still be serious First Amendment problems to consider in any attempts legally to control violent media, there is more justification for feminist concern in that area. Currently in the United States there are no legal prohibitions on violence in media, while there are many legal constraints on representations of sex in media. What possible justification can there be for seeking more restrictions on the sexually explicit, while leaving the vast quantities of media violence unmolested?

Is Porn a 'Documentary of Abuse'?

Catharine MacKinnon has argued that pornography is a literal photographic record of women being abused. She has listed various images found in porn, such as women being bound, tortured, humiliated, battered, urinated upon, forced to eat excrement, killed, or 'merely taken and used'. She has then concluded that a woman had to have had these things done to her in order for the pornography to have been made; thus for each such image some woman had been bound, tortured, humiliated, battered, urinated upon, forced to eat excrement, murdered, or 'merely taken and used'.[32] Or as Andrea Dworkin puts it, 'Real women are tied up, stretched, hanged, fucked, gang-banged, whipped, beaten, and begging for more. In the photographs and films, real women are used …'[33] In this view, pornography is a photographic record of horrible abuse perpetrated upon the models and actors who appear in it. Several points may be made about this theory of pornographic harm.

The items on such lists are not all equivalent nor are they equally prevalent. I would guess that the 'merely taken and used' is in reference to ordinary, non-kinky sexual activities, while the items bound, tortured, humiliated, urinated upon and forced to eat excrement may refer to kinky porn. Porn featuring the eating of excrement is extraordinarily rare. Images of bondage, pain, humiliation and urination are found in porn but, again, are absent from the majority of pornography. I have heard references to porn showing women mutilated or murdered but have never seen any except some rare drawings – *not* photographs – in European materials not available in the United States. I hate to belabour the point, but there are more women battered and murdered on prime-time television and Hollywood films than in pornographic materials.

Perhaps more significantly, in this model of porn there is no concept of the role of artifice in the production of images. We do not assume that the occupants of the vehicles routinely destroyed in police chases on television are actually burning along with their cars, or that actors in fight scenes are actually being beaten to a pulp, or that western movies result in actual fatalities to cowboys and native Americans. It is ludicrous to assume that the level of coercion in an image is a reliable guide to the treatment of the actors involved. Yet this is precisely what is being asserted with regard to pornographic images.

In their characterizations of pornography as a documentary of abuse, both Dworkin and MacKinnon appear to think that certain sexual activities are so inherently distasteful that no one would do them willingly, and therefore the models are 'victims' who must have been forced to participate against their will. Since SM often involves an appearance of coercion, it is especially easy to presume that the people doing it are victims. However, as I noted above, this is a false stereotype and does not reflect social and sexual reality. Sadomasochism is part of the erotic repertoire, and many people are not only willing but eager participants in SM activity.[34]

However, sadomasochism is not the only behaviour subjected to condescending and insulting judgements. For example, MacKinnon has also described porn in which someone was 'raped in the throat where a penis cannot go'.[35] There are plenty of gay men, and even a good number of heterosexual women, who enjoy cock-sucking. There are even lesbians who relish going down on dildos. Obviously, oral penetration is not an activity for everyone, but it is presumptuous to assume that it is physically impossible or necessarily coercive in all circumstances. Embedded in the idea of porn as a documentary of abuse is a very narrow conception of human sexuality, one lacking even elementary notions of sexual diversity.

The notion of harm embodied in the MacKinnon/Dworkin approach is based on a fundamental confusion between the content of an image and the conditions of its production. The fact that an image does not appeal to a viewer does not mean that the actors or models experienced revulsion while making it. The fact that an image depicts coercion does not mean that the actors or models were forced into making it.

One can infer nothing from the content of an image about the conditions of its production. Any discussion of greater protections for actors and models should focus on whether or not they have been coerced and on the conditions under which their work is performed *regardless of the nature of the image involved.* Any standards considered for the health, safety or cleanliness of working conditions in the sex industry should conform to those pertaining to similar occupations such as fashion modelling, film making, stage acting, or professional dancing. The content of the image produced, whether or not it is sexual, and whether or not it is violent or distasteful to a viewer, is irrelevant.

While anti-porn activists often claim to want to protect women in (and from) the sex industry, much of their analysis is based on condescension and contempt towards sex workers. The notion that pornography is a documentary of sexual abuse assumes that the women who work in the sex industry (as strippers, porn models or prostitutes) are invariably forced to do so and that such women are merely victims of 'pornographers'. This is a malignant stereotype and one that is especially inappropriate for feminists to reinforce.

There are, of course, incidents of abuse and exploitation in the sex industry, as there are in all work situations. I am not claiming that no one has ever been coerced into appearing in a porn movie or that in such cases the perpetrators should not be prosecuted. I am saying that such coercion is not the industry norm. Furthermore, I am not promoting a simple 'free choice' model of employment, in which structural forces and limited choices have no influence on what decisions individuals make about how to earn a living. But those who choose sex work do so for complex reasons, and their choices should be accorded the respect granted to those who work in less stigmatized occupations.

Indeed, the degree to which sex workers are exposed to more exploitation and hazardous working conditions is a function of the stigma, illegality or marginal legality of sex work. People in stigmatized or illegal occupations find it difficult to obtain the protections, privileges and opportunities available for other jobs. Prostitutes, porn models and erotic dancers have less recourse to police, courts, medical treatment, legal redress or sympathy when they are subjected to criminal, violent or unscrupulous behaviour. It is more difficult for them to unionize or mobilize for protection as workers.

We need to support women wherever they work. We need to realize that more stigma and more legal regulation of the sex industry will merely increase the vulnerability of the women in it. Feminists who want to support sex workers should strive to decriminalize and legitimize sex work. Sex workers relieved of the threat of scandal or incarceration are in a better position to gain more control over their work and working conditions.[36]

Contempt towards sex workers, especially prostitutes, is one of the most disturbing aspects of the anti-porn invective. Throughout her book, *Pornography*, Dworkin uses the stigma of prostitution to convey her opprobrium and make her argument against pornography. She says, 'Contemporary pornography strictly and literally conforms to the word's root meaning: the graphic depiction of *vile whores*, or in our language, *sluts*, *cows* (as in: *sexual cattle, sexual chattel*), *cunts*.'[37] This is a degrading and insulting description of prostitutes. Feminists should be working to remove stigma from prostitution, not exploiting it for rhetorical gain.

Is Porn at the Core of Women's Subordination?

Porn is often described as 'at the centre' or 'at the core' of women's subordination. Andrea Dworkin makes the following statement in *Right-Wing Women*:

> At the heart of the female condition is pornography: *it is the ideology that is the source of all the rest*; it truly defines what women are in this system – and how women are treated issues from what women are. Pornography is not a metaphor for what women are; it is what women are in theory and in practice.[38]

This rather extraordinary statement is accompanied by several diagrams in which pornography is first placed literally 'at the centre' of women's condition, then diagrammed as the underlying ideology of women's condition, and finally depicted as the surface phenomenon with prostitution the underlying system.[39] These are breathtaking claims, and they are made with little supporting evidence and not a single citation.

Since the 1960s, feminist theorists and academics have explored a multitude of explanations for female subordination and the oppression of women. There are hundreds of articles, essays and books debating the merits of various factors in the creation and maintenance of female subordination. These have included, for example, private property, the formation of state societies, the sexual division of labour, the emergence of economic classes, religion, educational arrangements, cultural structures, family and kinship systems, psychological factors, and control over reproduction, among others. I cannot think of a single attempt prior to the porn debates to derive women's subordination from either pornography or prostitution. There is no credible historical, anthropological or sociological argument for such a position.

It would be difficult to argue that pornography or prostitution had played such critical roles in women's subordination since women are quite dramatically oppressed in societies that have neither (for example, sedentary horticulturalists in Melanesia and South America). Furthermore, pornography and prostitution as they now exist in the west are modern phenomena. The institutional structures of prostitution in, for example, ancient Greece, were entirely different from those that obtain today.

Pornography in the contemporary sense did not exist before the late nineteenth century. Other cultures have certainly produced visual art and crafts depicting genitalia and sexual activity (e.g. the ancient Greeks, the Egyptians, and the Moche Indians from pre-Columbian coastal Peru). But there is no systematic correlation between low status for women and cultures in which sexually explicit visual imagery exists, or high status for women and societies in which it does not. Moreover, such images are not pornography unless porn is to be defined as all sexually explicit imagery, in which case anti-porn ideology would posit the impossibility of any acceptable explicit depictions of sex, and few feminists would support it.

Pornography could be thought of as being at the heart of women's condition if it is conceptualized as a trans-historical category existing throughout human history and culture. In *Pornography*, Dworkin states that the word 'pornography' comes from Greek words meaning 'writing about whores'. She goes on to discuss the place of the 'whores' in Greek society and concludes that, 'The word pornography does not have any other meaning than the one cited here, the graphic depiction of the lowest whores.' From this discussion, and similar accounts by others, it has often been inferred that the term 'pornography' was used by the Greeks and that it refers to categories of Greek experience.[40]

However, the term 'pornography' was not used by the ancient Greeks, did not refer to their painted vases, and should not be treated as evidence that the Greeks felt about porn the way Dworkin does. The term was coined *from Greek roots* in the nineteenth century, when many of the sex terms still in use (such as homosexuality) were assembled from Greek and Latin root words. It embodies not the prejudices of the Greeks, but those of the Victorians.[41]

There is one further sense in which it might be argued that pornography is 'the ideology that is the source of all the rest' of women's oppression, and that is if pornography is conceived of as the quintessence of all ideologies of female inferiority. What, then, are we to make of all the religious and moral and philosophical versions of male superiority? Is the Koran pornography? The Bible? Psychiatry? And what has any of this to do with modern, contemporary commercial porn? What has it to do with adult bookstores or *Playboy*?

IV Why Has Opposition to Pornography Been So Acceptable in Feminism?

One may wonder why such sloppy definitions, unsupported assertions and outlandish claims have gained so much credibility within the feminist movement. There are several explanations.

1.   Pornography is already highly stigmatized in this society. This stigma certainly pre-dates feminist attention to the subject. Most people in this society are already uncomfortable with pornography and a little afraid of being contaminated with its aura of disrepute. For well over a century the safest and most respectable attitude towards sexually explicit media has been one of condemnation. This stigma of pornography also makes it easier for people to accept false statements about it. One could assemble all the most grotesque slasher films or offensive paperback fiction and try to incite feminist frenzy against movies houses or bookstores, but few feminists would take such a campaign seriously.

2.   It is often easy for women to accept hyperbolic descriptions of pornography because most women who do not work in the sex industry are unfamiliar with pornographic materials and their conventions of meaning and interpretation. Traditionally, pornography has been male territory. 'Respectable' women did not get much opportunity to go into porn shops and theatres or to view pornography.

Men's behaviour around porn – often embarrassed, furtive, and uncomfortable – has done little to change this situation or to reassure women about what might be going on in those male enclaves. Many women are angry and resentful about men's privileged access to sexually explicit material. All of this is changing, as the women who work in the sex industry are becoming more outspoken and as the industry itself evolves. The video revolution has enabled women to rent movies and view them in the comfort of their own homes. More women are becoming comfortable in adult theatres and bookstores.

3. Most pornography *is* sexist. Traditionally, it has been aimed at a male audience and at the values of mainstream men. Consequently, the women in most commercial porn really are there to represent what the average male consumer wants to think about when he is masturbating. Most pornography does misrepresent women's sexuality and does not encourage men to learn the arts of seduction or to think of their sex partners as independent people with their own needs.

However, this sexism is no more intrinsic to pornography than it is to fiction. It is already changing as more women have become involved with the production of porn. Furthermore, the porn industry is beginning to recognize women as potential consumers and to design products intended to appeal to a female audience.

4. Commercial porn does not pretty-up sex the way Hollywood movies do. Most porn is poorly produced, badly acted, too brightly lit, and shot on too low a budget. It looks cheap. In spite of all the tripe about porn being a multi-billion dollar megalith, most porn movies are shot on budgets that would barely dent the cosmetic allowance for a major Hollywood film. The actors are not always well trained, and few have the impeccably good looks of major film stars. Many people come to porn expecting it to have the visual appearance of big screen romance, and it quite regularly fails to meet such expectations.

5. In this society we do not often get to view people who are nude or engaging in fornication or other sex acts. Most people consequently feel that sex looks kind of silly, and are afraid they must look ridiculous when they do it. Anti-porn ideology manipulates such feelings and reinforces the message that unadorned sex is ugly, undignified and shameful.

6. Due to the stigma historically associated with sexually explicit materials, we already use the words 'obscene' and 'pornographic' to express many kinds of intense revulsion. For example, war may be 'obscene' and Reagan's policies 'pornographic'. However, neither is customarily found in adult bookstores. Since the terms are commonly used to convey profound and extreme disapproval, it is all too easy to utilize them to invoke anxiety, disgust and revulsion.

7. There are legitimate feminist concerns with regard to sexually explicit materials. Although pornography should not be singled out, it should not be immune from feminist criticism. Porn is certainly not uniformly pleasing, well produced, artistically

edifying or politically advanced. There is plenty of room for improvement and for porn that is well made, creative, more diverse, more attuned to women's fantasies, and more infused with feminist awareness. This will only happen as more women and more feminists become involved in the production of sexually explicit material. A feminist politics on pornography should be aimed at making it easier – not more difficult – for this to occur.

As I mentioned above, the women who work in the sex industry are more vulnerable to harassment, violence and exploitation because they are denied many of the protections readily available to others. A feminist politics on the sex industry should demand immediate decriminalization of prostitution and pornography, equal protection under the law for sex workers, and an end to the punitive stigma inflicted upon people in the industry.

V Costs and Dangers of Anti-porn Politics

The focus on pornography trivializes real violence and ignores its gravity. Experiences of being raped, assaulted, battered or harassed are dramatic, devastating and qualitatively different from the ordinary insults of everyday oppression. Violence should never be conflated with experiences that are merely upsetting, unpleasant, irritating, distasteful, or even enraging.

Anti-porn activity distracts attention and drains activism from more fundamental issues for women. Porn is a sexier topic than the more intractable problems of unequal pay, job discrimination, sexual violence and harassment, the unequal burdens of child-care and housework, increasing right-wing infringements on hard-won feminist gains, and several millennia of unrelenting male privilege vis-a-vis the labour, love, personal service and possession of women. Anti-porn campaigns are pitifully misdirected and ineffective. They cannot solve the problems they purport to address.

If anti-porn politics were only a trivial diversion from more important concerns they would not deserve so much critical attention. This is unfortunately not the case. There are real costs to these campaigns that will be paid by whole new classes of victims. The scapegoating of pornography will create new problems, new forms of legal and social abuse, and new modes of persecution. A responsible and progressive political movement has no business pursuing strategies that will result in witch-hunts.

Anti-porn politics scapegoat innocent but despised behaviours, media and individuals for problems for which they are not responsible. Anti-porn politics are intended to result in increased stigma and increased legal persecution of pornography, prostitution and perversion. But these are neither abstractions nor monsters. The consequences of more criminalization of sexually explicit materials and of increased stigmatization of sexual variation are very real. They mean police abuse and bureaucratic harassment for women and men who have done nothing wrong but express unfashionable desires, create illicit imagery or engage in disreputable occupations.

It is a terrible thing to bring down the police, public hatred and bureaucratic intervention upon innocent communities or individuals. It is inappropriate and shameful for feminism to collude in establishing policies, attitudes and law that will deprive innocent women and men of their liberty, livelihoods and peace of mind. Feminists are under the same obligations as everyone else to remember that just because something seems strange or frightening does not mean it is dangerous or a menace to public safety.

Anti-porn feminists are playing into the hands of the right wing and its reactionary agenda. There may not be a direct conspiracy, but there is certainly a convergence of aims and intentions. At best, anti-porn feminists seem naive about the political context in which they are operating. The right has already adopted feminist anti-porn rhetoric, concepts and language, conveniently stripped of its already marginal progressive content.

The women's movement lacks the political capacity to enact any legislative programme on pornography at this time. The right is suffering no such limitation. The right is more powerfully entrenched in the political structure of the United States than it has been in decades. It wields the formidable power of the federal bureaucracy and has enormous influence on legislative activity at all levels of government. We can expect a wave of conservative legislation on pornography to pass at the local, state and federal levels in the next few years. It is especially likely that laws loosely modelled on the concepts of the MacKinnon/Dworkin ordinance but wedded to traditional obscenity standards will become common.[42] Moreover, everything we have seen so far will have been a prelude to the legislative avalanche we can expect once the Meese Commission on pornography reports.[43]

These are times of great danger. We are in a period in which the social attitudes and legal regulation of sexuality are undergoing massive transformation. The laws, policies and beliefs that are established in this era will haunt feminism, women, sex workers, lesbians, gay men and other sexual minorities for decades.

VI Feminism and Sexual Politics

It is tragic that the feminist movement has already fed the gathering sexual storm. The anti-porn ideology in all its manifestations has damaged the women's movement as a progressive voice in sexual politics. It has far too often paralysed feminist response to right-wing encroachments. It is critical that the women's movement mobilize to oppose any further depredations on sexual freedoms.

Instead of fighting porn, feminism should oppose censorship, support the decriminalization of prostitution, call for the abolition of all obscenity laws, support the rights of sex workers, support women in management positions in the sex industry, support the availability of sexually explicit materials, support sex education for the young, affirm the rights of sexual minorities and affirm the legitimacy of human sexual diversity. Such a direction would begin to redress the mistakes of the past. It would restore feminism to a position of leadership and credibility in matters of sexual policy. And it would revive feminism as a progressive, visionary force in the domain of sexuality.

2

The Primarolo Bill

In Britain, some feminists have attempted to introduce anti-pornography legislation, using the same vague new definition of pornography promoted by Andrea Dworkin and Catharine MacKinnon in their ill-fated attempts to create laws against pornography in the US. Bristol MP Dawn Primarolo has been campaigning for such a bill, the purpose of which appears to be to prevent bookstores and newsagents from carrying soft-core magazines like *Penthouse* and *Mayfair*, and to discourage newspapers like the *Sun* from printing photographs of unclad models, but which would in fact make it illegal to sell sexual material even in Britain's sex shops. This law would create a new category of shop and licence for Britain – the porn shop – and would empower Trading Standards Officers to be the arbiters of our tastes.

Location of Pornographic Material Bill (Primarolo)
A BILL TO Provide for the licensing of premises for the location of pornographic material; to create an offence of locating pornography on unlicensed premises; to extend the duties of Trading Standards Officers; and for connected purposes.

BE IT ENACTED by the Queen's most Excellent Majesty, by and with the advice and consent of the Lords Spiritual and Temporal, and Commons, in this present Parliament assembled, and by the authority of the same, as follows:

1. (1) It shall be an offence to display, sell or otherwise distribute any pornographic material from any premises unless the vendor or distributor has a licence to sell or distribute such material from those premises; or, as the proprietor of such premises, to permit such unlicensed display, sale or distribution.

   (2) It shall be an offence to display, sell or otherwise distribute pornographic material to the general public from premises where any other goods or services whatsoever are sold; or, as the proprietor of such premises, to permit such display, sale or distribution.

(3) A licence to sell or otherwise distribute pornographic material shall be granted only by the appropriate local authority for the area where the premises are situated, and a licence shall be granted only where the premises from which material is sold or distributed are used solely for the sale or distribution of pornographic material.

2. (1) Any person guilty of an offence under this Act shall be liable

   (a) on summary conviction to a fine not exceeding level five on the Standard Scale or to imprisonment for a term not exceeding six months or both; or

   (b) on conviction on indictment, to a fine or imprisonment or both;

   and the court may order that the premises used for sale or distribution of pornographic materials may be closed.

3. (1) Pornographic material means film and video and any printed matter which, for the purposes of sexual arousal or titillation, depicts women, or parts of women's bodies, as objects, things or commodities, or in sexually humiliating or degrading poses or being subject to violence.

   (2) The reference to women in sub-section (1) above includes men.

We hope it is lost on no one that the true effect of this bill will be virtually to eliminate what little sexual material is now sold legally in Britain. The definition of pornography used above can refer to any sexual depiction of any person, male or female, no matter how tightly the women who promote that definition *think* it defines 'pornography'. It will affect most gay periodicals, many ordinary feminist works, and will mean that women and gay men will have to go to these 'porn shops' if they want to see material that is deemed pornographic (by the police and courts, naturally – feminists will not be consulted about who is charged or the materials involved).

Of course, this assumes that the porn shops will exist at all, which is another matter. Sex shops in Britain currently carry limited forms of pornography and also survive by selling lingerie, sex toys and related matter. It is debatable whether they could survive economically on the pornography alone, severely limited as it is, and of course the currently existing sex shops would have to stop selling pornography if they wanted to sell 'any other goods', as they do now – or, it must be remembered, if the councils declined to give them licences for the sale of pornography.

In the last ten years, councils have shown a decided reluctance to licence sex shops, and many such shops have been closed down by councils as a result of the repressive campaigns. What is the likelihood that these same councils will now grant licences for the new porn shops that this bill calls for? We think those chances are vanishingly small, and the result would be that no shop owner of any kind will be able or willing to take the risk of carrying publications with even the tamest sexual content, given the penalties involved if they are deemed to be 'pornographic' under the terms of this bill.

Was this Primarolo's true intent? She has claimed sympathy with the gay community, and also portrays herself as a feminist, but it takes little imagination to see the disastrous effect this bill will have on feminist and gay materials. If she truly meant to get soft-core magazines and photos out of the newsagents, why doesn't the bill simply limit those materials to the sex shops as they are currently licenced? How does she explain the unnecessary and dangerous extension of Trading Standards Officers' powers? And why has she rebuffed the many attempts by gay, feminist and anti-censorship organizations to open dialogue about these questions?

This dangerous piece of censorship has had support from a substantial number of Primarolo's fellow Labour MPs. Ominously, a number of Conservative MPs wrote to the Prime Minister in the summer of 1991 expressing their support for this bill and requesting that similar goals be made part of the party platform in the coming election. Yet the outrage we would have expected to hear from the press, the publishing industry in general, and from civil libertarians has been strangely muted. In fact, many affected shopowners have proven to be entirely ignorant of this threat to their business. Where are the voices in support of freedom?

3

The First Amendment to the Bill of Rights of the United States Constitution

As the US Constitution's First Amendment is mentioned several times in this book, we thought we would give you its entire text. Judge for yourself whether you think laws against pornography violate the right granted herein – a point many judges, legislators and legal scholars can not agree on.

> Congress shall make no law respecting an establishment of religion, or prohibiting the free exercise thereof, or abridging the freedom of speech, or of the press; or the right of the people peaceably to assemble, and to petition the Government for a redress of grievances. This right is either absolute or it does not exist.

4

Changing Perceptions in the Feminist Debate

AVEDON CAROL AND NETTIE POLLARD

Double standards make good bandits
that strip us of our pride.

P.F. Sloan

Over the last decade or so the emphasis on certain words and concepts as used in some parts of the feminist movement seems to have shifted out of an analytical mode into a largely prescriptive and proscriptive one. This emphasis seems to be most strongly expressed in the anti-pornography movement that has become a most vocal and public aspect of the feminist movement, and the new definitions creeping into the feminist discourse have sometimes obliterated the initial insights that brought such useful terms into being.

In the early days of the women's liberation movement, a lot of us discussed examples of men treating women as 'objects': we were often pursued by men we had not really met, who had simply taken one look at us and decided that we now were obliged to satisfy their interests; some of us had dated men who had clearly been attracted to us because we were independent and 'different from other women', but who then proceeded to try to shoe-horn us into stereotypical wifely roles that had nothing to do with our interests and personalities; in the workplace, we were – and are – often made acutely aware that our femaleness seems to define our job requirements, and 'femininity' generally controls whether we get jobs at all. Most blatantly, some men actually stated publicly that they had no interest in any woman who was not a potential sexual partner.

The definition of 'objectification' in current use in the anti-pornography debate appears to have changed from the original meaning feminists applied to it in the early days of the modern feminist wave. The new application is often brought up to define the alleged negative possibilities of pornography, but seems to overlook the essential definitions that gave 'objectification' meaning as a feminist term, with the result that now human sexuality is re-defined to suit these purposes.

The original terminology referred to the evaluation of individual women in terms of their sexual function and attractiveness, using people as objects without reference to mutuality, and projecting male-defined fantasies or idealized versions of the feminine on to real, living, breathing women.

In London today, any woman may see several free magazines a week – *Ms London, Girl About Town, Midweek,* etc. – in which advertisements for secretaries and personal assistants place youth and 'smart' or 'pleasing' appearance in such priority that you can't help the feeling that you're really looking at sex ads and that 'secretary' is actually a euphemism for 'mistress'. Once a woman gets into the job – whether it is a secretarial position or a more highly-regarded technical job such as computer programmer, and even up to the executive level – she finds she is expected to perform sex role-defined functions like making coffee for the men in the office. Although some women feel discomfort at these things, few seem able to articulate that this is sexual harassment and the soil from which it grows; we are expected to accept and cater to male insistence that we perform a sex-object function in the workplace. It is curious that so few feminists in Britain today recognize these things for what they are.

Men sometimes feel free to criticize the appearance of women they barely know – a man will ask why a woman doesn't dress 'more like a woman,' or tell her she should smile more, for example. Movies have often shown men walking up to women in offices and laboratories and removing their glasses and hair pins to make them look more 'feminine' and 'show them' that they can be 'womanly'. On the screen and in the streets, perceptions of a woman's attractiveness override any recognition of her capabilities or individuality as a real person; lesbians seen as attractive are 'a waste', and any woman who does not make an effort to please men by behaviour and appearance is simply an outrage. Our failure to consider our attractiveness to men over any other considerations is treated as inadequate, anti-social or ignorant. In these days of so-called 'post-feminism', this role is institutionalized in the workplace and, in fact, is sometimes less present in our private lives than it is in our working[1] lives. We are actually turned into sexual objects in the inappropriate atmosphere of the office, for example, to an extent that many women do not experience in the bedroom. In other words, we have constant reminders that we are obliged to look nice for men and be nice to men, that retaining object status is part of our *job* as women. (In fact, this is more true today than it was back when hard-core pornography was widely available; women who work in offices today are now expected to dress and make themselves up in ways that only women who were actors, models or prostitutes were expected to do 20 years ago.)

The original definition of sexual objectification by feminists encompassed not only the idea that women should make themselves objects for men, but also challenged the definition of 'attractive' as young, slim, blonde and not too bright. The early rejection of objectification was an assertion of a woman's right to her own sexual identity and to her own sexual freedom.

The new meaning given to 'objectification' seems to have eliminated most of this political analysis and disregarded the basic interpersonal dynamics involved. It now seems to have devolved to mean merely finding women physically attractive and admiring the physical attributes of a woman or women, and looking at women or pictures of women sexually. This usage is applied between women as well as to men, and is sometimes reversed to apply to women who like to look at men's bodies or even pictures of their own lovers. The assumption is made that if one finds a particular physical feature of one's lover, or of any woman or man, compelling, one is therefore devaluing them as a whole person.

This new definition sits comfortably with a suspicious and negative attitude towards sex that currently seems to be re-establishing itself in the general culture, and which contradicts the initial feminist objective of a self-defined and self-directed sexuality for women. Where once feminists recognized that women's sexuality had been other-defined, and that we should be freed from this outward restriction on who and what we were, we now seem to be accepting newly narrowed re-definitions of our sexuality which encourage an attitude of paternalistic protectiveness toward women and children. The de-sexualization of women, so familiar from Victorian ideology, seems to have resurfaced in the guise of feminist analysis.

This curious re-definition of a once useful word is disturbing to those of us who still wish to analyse and uproot a more complex system of sexist oppression. The older definition more thoroughly recognizes the inherent failures of a society in which actual, individual women are treated not only as sex objects, but as nurturant objects, romantic objects, 'mother-of-my-children' objects, support objects (as exemplified in 'women's work'), and representatives of 'good womanhood'. Women are objectified by the society as a whole in the routine maintenance of stereotyping and generalizing from stereotypes to real people in absolute terms. This process goes far beyond the simple matter of finding some secondary sexual characteristics appealing. The objectification of women fulfils a clear function in the maintenance of male power. It identifies women as objects, not subjects – as second class. It defines women not only by our gender, but measures us by how desirable we can appear to men and how well we serve the nurturing functions and maintenance work in sexism's fundamental institution: the family.[2]

In fact, the entire analysis in which specifically female characteristics are being rejected as identifiably attractive is in itself a curious deviation from the fundamentals of feminism, and should be looked on with some suspicion at a time like this when biologically determined female traits (most dramatically, higher levels of body fat) are also being rejected and degraded in the general society. Is it really any accident that women's curves are being devalued in fashion and the culture at large at the same time that feminists are downgrading the appreciation of those traits? And does it make any sense, when we are trying to identify the authentic sexuality of women, to deny that we (women, humans) do react to the physicality of our lovers?

The women's movement has made men very insecure in relation to women. The anti-fat/anti-curves fashion has gone hand-in-hand with men feeling comfortable with their women wearing clothes that project a less passive sexuality. Many men feel less threatened if women look boyish. Men feel threatened by big powerful women in a way they did not in the 1950s when sex roles were not really questioned.

Perhaps we have lost sight of our true interest in self-definition because we have also lost sight of another area of terminology that represented a crucial feminist insight: 'male-identification' and its reverse. Here, too, the meaning of the term has taken on new colours; worse, the alternatives have lost their true meaning altogether.

Identification with the oppressor, we have always known, has been a problem for all oppressed classes and castes. The same values promoted by the ruling group which degrade the subjected group become accepted by the victims of that ideology, so that now the oppressed people become unable to fight their way up because they, too, believe that they are inferior. Thus, we find that 'whiter'-looking black women are considered more attractive among blacks, for example.

Women, too, come to accept the web of double standards by which we are judged. The belief that men are smarter than women may not be as strong in the west as it once was, but it's not that long ago that this assumption was accepted by both women and men. This meant that our career failures were merely the result of our own lack of intelligence and skill, so we couldn't blame sexism (and the fact that we had been deliberately deprived of the necessary educational opportunities and qualifications or promotions) for it. Instead, we were supposed to feel complimented if we were judged 'pretty smart for a girl'.

At the same time we accepted the specific values by which women were judged – conventional attractiveness, 'femininity', home-making ability, whether we were 'nice' people. If we were capable of short tempers, anger, or normal human thoughtlessness, we were bad people and deserved to fail (despite the fact that 'aggressiveness' and single-mindedness were considered valuable business tools in men). If we were unhappy with the feminine role and starvation pay-cheques, it was because we were sexually dysfunctional, 'dykes', frigid, wanted to be men, or suffering from whatever the fashionable 'female problem' was at the time. Our misery and our failures were our own fault as individuals, and in no way reflected any general unfairness on the part of employers, husbands or society.

'Class consciousness' is, of course, the recognition that your oppression is *oppression*, and exists because you are stereotyped and dismissed as a member of an underclass, and *not* because of your own individual or group shortcomings. The first awakenings of class consciousness are a painful journey into rage for each individual who realizes, at last, how she has been not only ripped off, but made to believe that her exploitation is really perfectly all right, natural and acceptable, exactly what she has earned. When you realize that your 'personal' problems are in fact the symptoms of a deliberate political system, you have made your first break with being oppressor-identified.

In this sense, the reverse of 'male-identification' is group consciousness – the re-valuing of yourself and of the group to which you belong, breaking with the devaluation of yourself and your group that comes from the oppressor's values. To be 'woman-identified' is to recognize that the personal is political and that patriarchal society's perception of women as a purely sexual/nurturant/supportive service class is invalid and part of how we are kept from having power in society.

But women are 'male-identified' in another way: as women are defined in sexual terms, each of us is actually given an individual identity based not on who we are, but on who we have sexual relationships with. Since in this society we are assumed to relate sexually to men, this means that our identity is presumed to come from an individual man. We are also given subgroup identities that are based on whether or not we are the property of a particular man. Much like slaves in the antebellum south of the United States, we are given the names of our presumed masters: Sally Jones becomes Mrs Robert Smith. More than simply being *male*-identified, we are always *other*-identified.

The only appropriate form of identification for any woman is the same kind of identification that men are accorded automatically – one that makes no reference whatsoever to one's sexual availability or partnerships. This is why the term 'Ms' was retrieved from the old English dictionaries where it had lain dormant, and was dusted off for modern use: men are called by their own names and given the title 'Mr' because no one needs to know on first introduction whether they are married. 'Ms' means that women are self-identified – which is as it should be. (Indeed, why have titles at all? Why are we so keen to know someone's sex?)

Self-identification for individual women is crucial for many reasons, even leaving aside matters of personal dignity. The essence of stereotyping is that a restricted set of traits, tastes, interests and abilities is ascribed to every single individual within a caste, and no variation is allowed for individual personalities. To be oppressive a stereotype doesn't have to be false for *all* women; if it is true for most women but treated as true for every woman, it is dangerous to us and restricts our ability to express ourselves authentically. The process of stereotyping allows for exceptions only when they are re-defined to 'prove' the rule. Women who deviate from the accepted stereotypes are not treated as proof that women are different from each other or that the stereotype is wrong; instead, such women are seen as evidence that some females have become psychologically twisted in such a way that they are repressing their 'true' female interests and needs.

Some feminists, however, make this same mistake. They seem to have forgotten the need for self-identification and a self-motivated sexuality for women, preferring instead to replace 'male-identification' with a version of 'female-identification' which amounts to no more than the exchange of one identity substitute for another. There are even those who insist that women aren't really sexual. These women prescribe living and identifying with women (political lesbianism) as an antidote to the identification and valuing of women in men's terms, but this in no way gives women our own distinct identities. In fact, each woman's individual identity is still replaced with her definition in terms of a new idealized image of women – again based on sexual partnership.

These discussions of what women want and don't want all seem to seek a single definition of female thought and behaviour that reduces us down to a single stereotype, in which all women want and think the same things. No allowance is made for difference, and once again our validity as thinkers and actors hinges on how well we conform to the new stereotype of what women 'should' be.

Women have always been defined this way, so this is nothing new. Sexist social scientists before the 1970s spent a great deal of time explaining why no woman's testimony could be valid in describing her own needs and desires. If we had no memory of fantasizing sex with our fathers or of penis envy, this only proved that we 'suppress' our real feelings. If a woman said she had been sexually abused by her father, she was merely confusing fantasy with fact. Nowadays, some feminists insist that we can't like to look at pornography and we can't enjoy sex with men – or, in some cases, at all. Women who maintain that these descriptions of 'real women' do not fit their own experience are dismissed as 'brainwashed'. We even now have the spectacle of 'anti-sexist men' telling women what we should feel and think, because we are too oppressed to be able to think for ourselves. Once again, we are mere weak-minded women who have to be told what is best for us and protected from ourselves.

And so the worst aspects of paternalism masquerade as feminist thought. Like the sexologists and psychiatrists of the early part of this century, people who call themselves feminists and anti-sexists create a map of what an acceptable female should want and do, and we are all expected to conform to the map, even when it looks nothing like the 'territory' – us. We used to have consciousness-raising groups so that we could discuss our real feelings and give testimony to our authentic experience. Maybe we need them again to remind ourselves that we do not all fit to a politically comfortable standard that is defined by others.

It is this failure to address the variety of women's interests, experiece and abilities that has provided the most comfortable meeting ground for anti-feminists (fundamentalists, traditional anti-porn crusaders) and feminists in the anti-pornography movement. The less politicized women who support anti-pornography campaigns understand instinctively that any image of female sexuality can become an image with which they can expect to be compared, since difference in real women is generally treated only as a measure of how well or how poorly each woman exemplifies the feminine ideal. Pro-censorship feminists also recognize that any representation of a woman can – and often will – be treated as a representation of *all* women, rather than as simply one woman in a wider and highly varied female population. The insight these women have should not be dismissed; psychologists, poets, sociologists, and other social commentators and artists have demonstrated a consistent willingness to generalize about all women from as little as a single experience of one woman, or even from fictions about women. Andrea Dworkin, for example, uses the fictional Emma Bovary's sexual awakening as proof of the danger of woman's sexual pleasure (*Intercourse*, Secker & Warburg, 1987).

Women are not being unreasonable when they complain that men compare them (unfavourably) with women as represented in men's magazines. In fact, men and women often develop a very narrow idea of what kind of appearance and age is acceptably attractive in women, culled in large part from the even narrower depictions of 'beautiful' women that are portrayed in the media – all media. Certain men also demand sexual services from their wives or lovers because they have *heard* that other women do such things willingly (and pornography may provide some incidental confirmation). Since men can sometimes be expected to exhibit such atrocious behaviour, many women would just as soon limit any possible source of such unpleasant ideas, and this is one reason for the popularity of anti-porn crusades. However, it is the fact that men feel entitled to make these demands which is disgusting – not what they desire sexually. This is not caused by depiction of sex acts in pornography, but by a sexist society that does not afford women full human or sexual status. It should also be remembered that sex is not the only service that men demand from women in this way. Some men behave just as noxiously in regard to cooking and housework, for example.

Unfortunately, the reaction against pornography often takes the form of a denial that 'women' would ever engage willingly in any of the acts depicted in pornography. Theories abound that women can not really enjoy sex. Therefore, depictions of women enjoying oral sex or group sex, for example, mean that women are being misrepresented. This insistence on de-sexualizing women – a painfully familiar echo of the 1950s – is every bit as much a misrepresentation of real women as anything to be found in pornography. Yet its persistence should certainly tell us that there are many women out there for whom sex genuinely is an unpleasant experience.

There is no reason why women should take a positive attitude toward sex that is presented to us as a chore that we are required to perform for men. This is only the most easily recognized version of the assumption that women exist to supply others with service and comfort, and that we have no innate sexuality of our own. But if women continue to deny an authentic female interest in sex, how can sex be perceived any other way? If we persist in treating sex as something men must get from women whether *we* like it or not, we have already accepted the essence of female subordination to men's needs and service.

In other words, by accepting the de-sexualization of women, we promote the objectification of women. If sex is a necessary function that women dislike and men find irresistible, it is not really unreasonable for men to continue treating sex as a prize object in itself, to be bartered for, bought or stolen, without regard to the price women must pay for men's pleasure. In this context, we measure civilization by the degree to which men are 'gentlemen' about the means by which they trick women into providing sex for them or contract for it: how much money (directly, by prostitution, or indirectly, in marriage) and privilege will a man 'pay' to a woman in exchange for sex – or will he just rape or enslave her?

But of course, this is a stereotype – it does not represent the way most men and women feel or relate to each other, although it is precisely the image we were raised to believe in, where Our Man would protect us from servitude to others if we gave our intimate services exclusively into his ownership. Most men, like women, learn that this arrangement can never satisfy the desires they really feel for a mutual relationship. However, it is not surprising, in the wake of the earlier social purity movements and the modern anti-sex version of feminism that have both promoted this streotype, that some men waste their lives and those of the women they encounter in trying to act out this charade.

We cannot establish sexual balance between men and women unless we break through the myth that male sexual interest is stronger than female sexual interest. We must make plain that the negative feelings many women have towards sex are by no means proof that women can't enjoy sex, but rather result from the continued presentation of sex as something women must provide *for others* rather than as something we can do out of our own natural desires and for our own pleasures. And we are not going to be able to do that unless we are free to create art, entertainment, and documentary materials that deal specifically with this focus on sexuality. In the current climate, make no mistake, such material *will* be called pornography, by both traditionalists and by feminist anti-pornography campaigners.

Unfortunately, current restrictions on pornography and 'obscenity' make it difficult to portray sexuality as a mutual pleasure. In the United States, where much of the television and film shown in Britain originates, network broadcast standards have long forbidden all explicit sexual portrayal, and even where it is not explicit those standards specifically require that sex be shown as having negative consequences. This agenda is so wholly taken for granted in North America that the same values are commonly found even in art forms not so severely restricted as network television. Thus, the international airwaves are already heavily polluted with negative sexual messages.

In Britain, 'soft porn' suffers fewer display and distribution restrictions than 'hard core', and can be more widely disseminated – which is one reason why many people, particularly women, are far more familiar with soft core and generally assume that the same values are merely duplicated in hard core, only more brutally and graphically. But the definitions by which hard and soft porn are separated actually alter the very terrain that they may cover.

One distinction between the two forms prohibits pictures of lovers together in soft core, which means no mutuality can be portrayed. Full male erection is similarly unacceptable – and, in Britain, illegal. In other words, our definitions of obscenity and acceptability for news-stand distribution automatically eliminate the possibility of photographs that would portray men sexually and portray people as lovers rather than merely as models to be looked at.

Soft core also keeps to the same conventions of standards of beauty that are already established in the non-erotic media: thin women with flat bellies and symmetrical Aryan features (even in black women) are the rule. This is one of the aspects of pornography that most aggravates women – the unreality of the heavily stylized stereotype of attractiveness that is placed in such high value for all woman. Many anti-porn and pro-porn campaigners have complained that it is this insistence on holding women up to such an unrepresentative standard of 'beauty' that makes it so offensive. (Conversely, when these standards of beauty are not observed, complaints abound that the pictures are in bad taste – 'unattractive' or even 'perverted'.)

In many respects, the models in soft porn are de-sexualized by stylistic convention. They look thoroughly posed, and they are usually shown sweet, passive and smiling, waiting to be viewed. There is little else permitted in British soft core, and the models have few opportunities to demonstrate any more assertive or individual personality traits.

But hard core does not adhere to these same standards, and in many respects it is unfairly taking the rap for sins that are really more common to soft core (and to ordinary television and general-release film). Hard core shows a wider variety of female physical types, including women who are genuinely fat, women who have small breasts, and women who are older, shorter or taller than conventional models. A wider variety of facial types and racial features is seen in hard core, and even different patterns of body hair can be found – hairy legs, unshaven armpits, and sometimes even unplucked hair on the belly or breasts.

Since hard core allows the camera to focus on genitals and erections, men can be shown in the same way as women are shown, and this is often the case. Moreover, since men and women can be shown together, sex can be portrayed as mutual. In contrast to soft porn, hard core often shows women taking the initiative in sex, playing assertive and even dominant roles, and making clear that they are acting on their own wishes rather than those of others. The women in hard core tend to be stronger and are far less likely to appear submissive or passive.

In this context, many hard-core porn models can be perceived as playing a particularly exploited role only if the viewer assumes that only men can enjoy sexual activity. However, that pernicious assumption pervades society to the extent that even some feminists claim that all pornography shows women performing acts that we could never enjoy. Some feminist authors have written whole books to this effect, maintaining that every aspect of the sexual acts portrayed in pornography represents sexual interests and approaches that are unique to male psychology and contradict the true female personality, in which all such acts are unpleasant and abhorrent. It has even been asserted that all pornography is made by force or coercion, as no woman would willingly perform these acts.

This is a resurgence of the dualistic map of male and female personality that was popularized during the 1950s, when boys were 'snakes and snails and puppy-dogs' tails' and girls were 'sugar and spice and everything nice'. Anti-sex feminists promote the perception that women are innately unable to appreciate sexual physicality (including sexual intercourse), and that such appreciation is natural only to men and is essentially destructive – as with the old perception of men's 'beastly urges' that women were too 'refined' to share. Anti-feminists and other misogynists have always promoted the view that women have a more abstract and less physical sexuality than men, and that women are therefore the only people who can – and so *must* – control male arousal so that it will not surface in its ultimately animalistic and anti-social destructiveness; hence the need to be a 'good wife'.

But this dichotomous approach to male and female sexuality naturally promotes male exploitation of women and suppresses real female sexual expression. It assumes that male sexuality cannot be controlled by men themselves, thus leaving them with no responsibility for self-control and giving all such responsibility to women.[3] Moreover, it is so proscriptive for women that any attempt to investigate our own sexuality becomes unacceptable – we are expected to take the word of other feminists, if not the church, that we shouldn't be trying out new means of sexual expression because such things are wrong and we aren't supposed to like them anyway.

Nevertheless, we can not accept these restraints on women's sexual expression so early in the game. Our sexuality has always been defined for us by others. As yet, we have not learned enough about who we are and can be to identify *any* authentic female sexuality, let alone its limits. Our only legitimate option is to let each woman explore as she pleases and define for herself where she wishes to draw the line. We must not allow a new feminist orthodoxy to suppress our investigations and falsify our discourse out of fear that we might learn things about ourselves that we are afraid to know.

5

Mystery and Imagination: the Case of Pornography Effects Studies

ALISON KING

Introduction

During the late 1980s, anti-pornography crusaders in both the fundamentalist and radical feminist camps claimed that modern pornography effects research had proven a link between consuming pornography and the commission of sex crimes. As both groups believe that graphic representations of sex acts or genitalia constitutes a sex crime *per se*, the purpose of these references to 'science' was to win public support for their causes. Christian anti-vice crusaders have been using 'scientific' authorities to bolster their arguments for over 100 years. For radical feminists, this was a new departure, and a bizarre one. For a movement that has lambasted patriarchal 'science' as a misogynistic silencing of women's inner nature for over two decades, it is ironic that they now rest their public case for banning pin-up magazines on a positivistic reductive 'science'. For that is what most pornography effect studies are.

This short review will demonstrate that, given the way the research is conducted, it cannot be relied upon to make a judgement on anything, and that even if we were to take this research at face value, it has embarrassing implications for anti-pornography activists' belief systems.

For the purpose of this chapter, I will use the term 'pornography' as a shorthand to describe what Dr Bill Thompson refers to as: sexually orientated material of a graphic nature designed for recreation rather than education – the best non-judgemental definition around.

Methodological Misconceptions and Qualifications

Anti-pornography activists, even those with academic pretensions, clearly possess no more knowledge about the methodologies of pornography research, let alone psychosexual effects of sexually orientated material, than the general public. Readers should always consider the studies' methodologies before accepting or rejecting the results. To do anything else defeats the purpose of what is frequently a specific research project.

1 Clinical Terms

Before reading off scientific reports it is important to understand the language employed in the reports. Judging by their comments and articles, it is clear that anti-pornography popularizers do not realize that there is a difference between specific use of the terms 'arousal' and 'aggression' for behavioural psychologists who conduct most research, and the meaning the lay public give to these words. In particular the terms are not synonymous with sexual 'arousal' or sexual 'aggression'.

The nature of everyday physiological arousal raises two important qualifications regarding the use of pornography and inferring effects to that stimulus in pornography-aggression research.

2 The Clinical Method

The vast majority of experiments are conducted within the Buss Paradigm: participants (known as 'subjects') enter a laboratory where they are deliberately annoyed by a research worker. They are then shown some material – in this case pornography – and placed in a position where they can 'harm' the research worker, usually by pressing buttons that appear to deliver electric shocks, but which do not in reality. The subject does not know that the research worker is part of the experimental team. The experimental conditions can be manipulated by the research worker insulting or injuring the subject in order to make them angry and aggressive before exposure occurs – usually giving the subjects *real* electric shocks! The purpose of this procedure is to measure the 'effect' of the arousal stimulus upon the subjects' level of aggression, compared to another set of volunteers who have not been exposed to the stimulus – known as the 'control group'.

This procedure is justified by psychologists because they believe that a person's level of aggression is determined by two things: the amount of anger held against the target of their aggression, and the amount of physiological arousal possessed at the time.

Theories upon which clinical research rests argue that an external arousing stimulus can increase a subject's aggression.

This obviously means that *any* arousing stimulus will have a similar effect. If it did not, the applied theories could not assert it was the pornography that helped turn the subject's aggression into action. In other words, *any* form of arousal, not just pornography, will encourage pre-angered subjects to aggress (Zillmann, 1971). If the subject is not angered, the arousal stimulus will *not* encourage, let alone 'cause', the aggression.

This produces an obvious qualification to pornography research: as the subjects are angered, we can not state with certainty that any aggressive behaviour that follows is solely the result of exposure to the pornography; we are only observing potential effects. Would non-angered pornography consumers react in the same way?

The vital role of anger in aggression, and the deliberate creation of a predisposition toward aggression in these studies, is demonstrated by an ignored parallel phenomenon in aggression research called pro-social effects.

A person's level of pro-social behaviour (that is, being nice to people) is determined by their predisposition to be pro-social and their level of arousal at the time. As with aggression, a subject's pro-social behaviour will be increased by the amount of external arousal stimulus (Mueller and Donnerstein, 1981). The only female researcher in this area, Professor Kelley from NYSU at Albany, has demonstrated that male subjects exposed to pornography react faster to aiding a female victim perceived as suffering than subjects who had been exposed to non-sexual stimuli (K. Kelley et al., 1989). Przybyla also found that when two groups of subjects encountered a male or female experiment confederate with a problem, the male subjects in the group exposed to the sexually explicit material offered help more often and for longer than a control group not exposed to sexual material (Przybyla, 1985). The implications for pornography-aggression studies are obvious: experiments which demonstrate that pornography leads to violence do so because they are constructed in such a way that there can be no other outcome; if we change the options in the experiment we find that pornography can and does produce pro-social effects. These findings suggest that pornography as a stimulus does *not* determine aggression or pro-social effects *per se*; the effects depend, as they do with all other stimuli, upon the subjects' predispositions, not on the source of the arousal. Anti-pornography crusaders never quote Kelley's experiments.

3 Attitudinal Research

Experiments designed to test viewers' attitudes following consumption of pornography, determined by filling in questionnaires, suffer from two problems. First, even where attitudinal change is recorded, this does not mean that the viewer will turn that new attitude into action. Second, as the 'meanings' of the 'attitudes' recorded are invariably defined by the clinical psychologist rather than the viewer, even a reported attitude change has to be considered with some care. A subject's connotation of an answer may not match that of the researcher. As we shall see, these caveats are vital when considering the outcome of what has become a very simplistic means of testing post-consumption attitudes: asking the subject to give a verdict and sentence in a mock rape trial.

4 The Material Used

In the vast majority of reports researchers fail to provide readers with the exact title of the material used, preventing experimental replicability. Questionable assumptions by researchers regarding the content are rife. For example, the definition of an 8 mm 'stag film' as females being 'sexual objects for exploitation by men' (e.g. Zillmann and Bryant, 1984) implies that even within the context of the 'plot', the female can never be considered as deriving any pleasure from the experience – a somewhat sexist assumption. As we shall see, the subject's interpretation of material is vital, especially in experiments designed to test the existence and effect of rape myths prevalent among some males.

Researchers are not averse to changing the definition of content to suit their studies, either. In one group of experiments, Zillmann and Bryant insisted that women performers were portrayed as 'socially non-discriminating, as hysterically euphoric in response … and eager to accommodate seemingly any and every sexual request'. They then abandoned that interpretation in another series of experiments where the validity of the findings depended upon the material used being defined as showing women as sexually reluctant until coerced by males, but where the female discovers she 'enjoys' the experience (Zillmann and Bryant, 1984). This pair of researchers constantly appear oblivious to the fact that 'pornography' not only promotes different messages at different times, but the same material could be interpreted by viewers in many different ways. As a result, the researchers are imposing a structural meaning upon the content which the experimental subject may not share, and thereby prevent a unilateral interpretation of the experiment's results. Worse, they change that meaning at will to suit the purposes of their experiments. It should also be noted that, as the vast majority of research is conducted in America, results can hardly apply to Britain. When the Americans refer to 'soft core' or 'non-violent explicit material', this can mean anything from *Playboy* to material akin to *Colour Climax* (magazines) and *Swedish Erotica* (films and videos) that would be deemed 'hard core' and obscene in Britain.

5 Is it 'Science'?

To claim something is a 'scientific' fact requires an examination of the status of the research. While, collectively, researchers are using the best methodologies available within their field, the scientific validity of the research is debatable. The procedures used, especially when setting scales for tests, would not be accepted elsewhere in the 'scientific community'. Pornography research relies almost exclusively upon behavioural psychology, which cultural feminists reject in all other fields. Zillmann, for example, is convinced that he will find a link between aggression and pornography because a link between aggression and sex has been 'found' in rats (Zillmann, 1984)! These researches show no understanding of social construction of beliefs and actions whatsoever.

Even if we accept the validity of the Buss Paradigm, can clinical studies really support the implication that the material has an innate effect upon *all* males, at *all* times, leading to aggression against *all* women? In reality the studies are only viable when considering pornography's potential as an arousal stimulus, compared to others; the 'measurements' can not be used as self-evident explanation for the aggression level recorded.

In both the Buss Paradigm and 'attitude' testing, little or no account is given to the mental processes of the subjects or the control group. It is merely assumed that the input of the stimulus is the only difference between them. This is debatable, as is the motive behind the 'aggression' which follows.

Stanley Milgram's original experiment clearly demonstrated that subjects were quite willing to give a confederate what they thought were severe electric shocks because they wished to please the controller or see the experiment through, rather than because of a wish to exhibit aggression (Milgram, 1963). Others have suggested this obedience is the effect an authoritative college professor has on young students, the subjects in most tests. If these subjects had been questioned beforehand they would probably have expressed the moderately humane values of average American citizens, and would have denied the charge that they would torture people so easily. It should also be noted that, apart from the presence of the experimenter, there was no other stimulus in Milgram's study, let alone pornography; yet the students appeared aggressive. Also, when students are given a free choice to continue with the research and retaliate against the confederate who had aggressed against them, the vast majority of subjects take the option to leave and not aggress, despite being angered by the confederate (Fisher and Grenier, 1988).

In short, simplistic readings of experiments in aggression do not consider the questions of situational effects, motives, and the role of authority in the experiments.

6 Conflating Studies

Given the above qualifications it is extremely difficult, if not impossible, so readily to relate one set of findings to others as the anti-pornography lobby do; but there are more fundamental problems.

All anti-pornography lobby summaries of research rely upon what Bill Thompson has called 'top-lining': the tendency to read off the synopsis 'finding' of a study rather than examine the methodology and unjustified theoretical links often made therein. In doing so, anti-pornography crusaders commit one of the crassest errors imaginable. When researchers write up reports, they will include the results of several studies. Each one of those studies will have invariably included numerous experiments. To take an isolated finding from one of those experiments takes them out of the context of both the other experiments and the overall study.

Malamuth's famous study, demonstrating the existence of the male's Likelihood to Rape tendency, is a typical example of the manipulations of the activities and attitudes of the subjects involved to reach a behavioural conclusion, and how 'unscientific' such studies can be (Malamuth, 1984).

Malamuth's aim was to see if exposure to 'aggressive pornography' affects men's attitudes and subsequent behaviour towards women, and what mediating effect individual personal differences (determined by a self-reported propensity to rape) have on the effects of aggressive pornography. Therefore, he needed to establish the existence of a Likelihood to Rape factor (hereafter LR factor), which he attempted to secure by giving subjects a self-assessment form containing five options on a Likelihood to Rape scale ranging from (i) 'not at all likely to rape' to (iv) 'very likely to rape' – all, it must be noted, giving the subject the pre-condition that they could be assured of not being caught and punished. This raised immediate difficulties of validity.

The scale is obviously 'constraining' – four of the five scale points measure an increasing LR factor, but there is no opportunity to express a differentiation in a *no* Likelihood to Rape.

The form's wording presented another problem of interpretation. The connotations of the word 'rape' and its meaning for respondents was believed to be obvious. Yet it is the very fact that there is no agreement in society over 'rape' definition that aggrieves feminist theorists. Juries and the wider public clearly believe it should be judged situationally: how far both parties were culpable in what occurred, with the level of physical coercion treated as a major indicator of male intent (Amendolia and Thompson, 1991). While this produces a catch-22 for the victim, and we may not approve of this reasoning, how are we to read Malamuth's subjects' definition of rape? Were they using a version of the legal definition, or situational culpability, or even utilizing a radical feminist position? Whichever definition they were using, it did not denote an LR score anyway; it was an LR 'if I am not caught and punished' scale. What would the scores have been if the subjects were simply asked: what is your likelihood to rape? The LR scale, therefore, is merely a methodological tool; it does not by itself indicate these males' likelihood to rape.

Worse, the subjects completed their scales after they had been divided into three groups and exposed to three different conditions: one group after seeing a videotaped interview with an actual rape victim; one group after reading a pornographic description of rape; and one group with no experimental exposure at all. And yet, the differentiation in scores of these groups *are not* described in the report. All three sets were conflated to produce one set of figures. This method was justified by reference to 'a great deal of consistency' across these conditions (Malamuth, 1984, p. 22). Even if this were the case, this is clearly 'scientifically' unacceptable. It also produced a difficulty for Malamuth. As only 35 per cent of males reported any LR factor 'if guaranteed to avoid detection and punishment' at two or above on the five-point scale, and 20 per cent at three or above; 65 per cent of all males tested reported absolutely *no* LR factor, even when guaranteed they would avoid detection and punishment. Malamuth was in danger of losing over half his subjects, and the study too; the sample size would be too small to proceed.

To get around this problem, he designated the 35 per cent scoring two or more on the LR scale as having a *high* LR factor, irrespective of initial gradation, and those who declared *no* LR factor as having a *low* LR factor!

This manipulation of subjects' scores for the study's convenience may be viable for the purposes of the single experiment, but the implications of this re-coding for untrained eyes is obvious. A cursory reading of the study will imply that 35 per cent of men are potential rapists when this clearly was not the case. Furthermore, the vast majority of males who had no LR factor all will now be regarded as having a likelihood to do so.

In short, two erroneous research method strategies – proposing the unproblematic nature of rape and re-coding of the participants' responses to the scales – appear to produce a positive and useful measure for assessing not only real attitudes towards women, but also a measure of potential rape capability, when in reality they bear no relationship with the subjects' real responses. This has implications not only for Malamuth's methodology, but also for social policy.

The implication that *all* men do have a scientifically proven LR factor is exactly the 'evidence' popularizers like Dr Catherine Itzin have presented to the public! Dr Itzin runs the bizarrely named Campaign Against Pornography & Censorship and was instrumental in aligning separatist feminist organizations like Women Against Violence Against Women with reformist socialists like Clare Short in a united front against soft-core pornography. Their campaign literature relies heavily upon there being a link between sexual imagery and sexual violence. There is, however, no evidence for this view; on the contrary, the subjects in effect studies constantly demonstrate the opposite.

The ultimate test of 'science', of course, is the ability to replicate experiments. This is very difficult when the researchers rarely differentiate between the numerous experiments that make up the single 'study' referred to in their reports, that rarely contain enough details to replicate.

Yet, even when they overcame this problem, Fisher and Grenier, in a series of tests, failed to secure the same results when replicating the major experiments referenced by popularizers, despite using the same types of subject and material, creating the same pattern of exposure, and requiring subjects to complete the same questionnaires and tests (Fisher and Grenier, 1988). This failure suggests no studies to date have scientifically 'proven' validity.

7 Theoretical Considerations

If Malamuth's manipulations were not bad enough, the theoretical musings of the behaviouralists are both sexist and full of contradictions. As it is the researchers' theoretical views that enable them to make the inferences they make from their experiments, it is illuminating to look at the beliefs of Zillmann, the most popular researcher among the anti-pornography lobby.

Like many anti-pornography feminists, Zillmann believes that men, having consumed pornography, see women as 'meat' and as 'sex objects'. Such a view is simplistic, not scientific. Not only does it rely upon the unstated secular sin of 'objectification', it ignores the reality whereby it is possible to relate to the same person in different ways at different times. Zillmann can not admit this possibility, as behaviourists treat all men as the same.

Zillmann's claim to fame is his studies into the association between reading soft core and callous attitudes to women, which is justified by theoretical musings designed to mask the fact that his 20-year search to find a link between soft core and sexual violence had failed to prove anything. Instead, he argues that soft core promotes adverse attitudes that justify adverse behaviour. To do this he utilizes a concept of sex callousness, which rests not upon observable data but upon a theoretical construct to interpret data. He justifies his belief in the existence of sex callousness in the following way.

Zillmann dismisses biological 'imperatives' in explaining male and female approaches to sexual relations. He prefers biological 'abilities', suggesting men became choosers and takers, and women those chosen and taken, because men are stronger than women (Zillmann, 1989, p. 96). In doing so he ignores the contradiction of promoting a neo-biological *a priori* belief that males are innately prone to conflict resolution by violence. As he can not explain why, he offers the existence of cross-cultural sanctions against use of force in achieving sexual access to women (a further contradiction as all laws are manmade), and quotes Freud's belief that men have an 'urge' to overpower their sexual object because their persuasive skills took much longer to develop on an evolutionary time-scale. In other words, Zillmann would like us to believe that behaviour is socially constructed, but argues that men are violent and 'callous' towards women 'by nature'.

Having failed to explain this third contradiction, Zillmann suggests that the 'simple fact' that men in most cultures manage to refrain from using physical force with no ill effect to their well-being demonstrates that the sexual coercion of women is controllable rather than unavoidable (Zillmann, 1989, p. 98). Surely this demonstrates that men may not always feel violently inclined towards women, and that the existence of such laws demonstrates that the majority wish to prevent the minority using violence. Not for Zillmann. On the contrary, it's not law, but:

> the exploitation of the indicated ambiguities in consent signalling as well as the deliberate misinterpretation or neglect of expressed nonconsent that defines the domain of sex callousness. (Zillmann, 1989, p. 99)

Although law exists, the men demonstrate their callous behaviour by showing:

> disregard of, if not disrespect and contempt for, women's right to deny sexual access for whatever reason, at whatever time, and under whatever circumstances. Such disregard is what characterizes sexually callous men, and such men abound in contemporary western society. (Zillmann, 1989, p. 99)

In short, contemporary callousness is expressed in males' refusal to accept a woman's 'No Means No'. Surely Zillmann must admit that 'the use of anger and threat of violence' by men is relatively rare. So how does this non-violent callousness manifest itself in great abundance? Wait for it:

> breaking female resistance to [male] sexual advances with drugs (mainly by getting their dates drunk), deceit (false confessions of love), and threats (of discontinuance of relationships ...) (Zillmann, 1989, p. 99)

We dumb women are duped by callous men who buy us a drink, which so fuddles our brains we can not escape from their evil intent. Without even blinking, Zillmann reinforces this sexist and patronizing redefinition of coercion by quoting one study to insist that 23 per cent of American males cannot stop themselves attempting to obtain satisfaction once aroused, which amounts to violating the rights of women. Hold on: that means that 77 per cent of all men *can* and *do* 'control themselves' and respect 'women's rights', and do not possess a callous disposition. No wonder Zillmann quickly skates over this implication and refers us to the work of Mosher to assert that:

> The focal point of sex callous dispositions appears to be the perception of women and their sexuality. (Zillmann, 1989, p. 100)

Even if we accept this, clearly, the vast majority of men do not put this attitude into practice. Perhaps we should concentrate upon that 23 per cent who exhibit the real 'double standard' Zillmann inadvertently draws attention to, whereby:

> Callous dispositions are apparently 'justifiable' when they concern women who are very sexually active, especially with several male partners. Men behave as if they are entitled to sexual access with women who readily granted it to other men ... (Zillmann, 1989, p. 100)

This would make more sense, especially when that study also reveals that the 23 per cent also only recorded their likelihood to use force against certain 'types' of women – 'loose girls, gold-diggers, and teasers' – as opposed to 'loved and nice girls'. In short, Zillmann's own preferred data undermines his thesis of universal callousness. As we shall see below, the vast majority of studies seeking to determine rapists' motivations uncover similar attitudes and motives without realizing their importance. Professor Kelley has long recognized that it is men with 'conservative and stereo-typical' attitudes towards women who demonstrate aggressive and callous tendencies towards women.

Zillmann, however, fails to make the connection between this tendency and his insistence that the 'rape myth' – defined as the belief that 'No' does not mean 'No' because 'they like it really' – is the most self-serving justification of sexual coercion ever invented by callous men. As Zillmann is not completely blind – he gets a lot of research funds for his work – there must be a reason for ignoring the obvious inferences about callous attitudes being found in socialization rather than sexy pictures. There is: Zillmann wishes to assert that all pornography promotes the rape myth and is to blame for all sexually callous attitudes in society.

He does this by insisting that although macho attitudes are shaped in childhood – through the parents' encouragement of power, dominance, strength, toughness, competitiveness and aggression, and then reinforced by aggressive sports and peer group 'delinquency' – its major outlet is found in dominance of females in sex. He does not bother to explain why this 'hyper-masculinity' does not remain in other outlets like competitive sports, or how controlling a 'powerless, submissive, weak, feeble, uncompetitive and non-aggressive' female increases one's masculinity rating in the eyes of other males, let alone why 77 per cent of men apparently escape this attitude. What he does say, however, is that men are encouraged in their behaviour by the fact that women are known to be attracted to uncultured, callous, macho men. Apart from providing no evidence for this statement, the implications are ironic, to say the least. If what Zillmann says is true, women would appear to demonstrate that the rape myth, given Zillmann's description of callous behaviour above, would not be a myth at all! But wait, there is more: Zillmann then exonerates society and capitalism from all blame for sexual callousness, for callousness is not reinforced by 'macho values' exercised in the business world or the professions:

> Men's callousness is specific to the welfare of women, and their sexual callousness is specific to women's behaviour in the sexual arena. (Zillmann, 1989, p. 103)

This somewhat contentious 'feeling' is based upon two beliefs: first, the decline of institutional rites of passage has given way to pornography as the primary male means of sexual 'indoctrination'; second, pornography promotes callous perceptions of female sexuality. Social reinforcement from peers, apparently, is hardly necessary, and superfluous.

Apart from simplistically ignoring over a century of anthropological and sociological inquiry into sexual habits, Zillmann can provide no evidence that pornography is the major source of male socialization regarding women. And even if it were, where is his content analysis to justify the assertion that it promotes callousness? To say that all pornography does so is to predetermine what its 'message' is.

More intriguing is the assertion regarding the lack of business or professional callousness. Why was Zillmann so concerned to make this blatantly sexist comment, which assumes that all business and professional personnel worthy of note are men? Has he never heard of war, torture, or economically promoted famines?

Zillmann's major rationale appears to be that pornography emphasizes short-term and instrumental sex, and that is callous. Why, we are not told. Even though he admits that soft-core depictions of sex acts tend to be mutual and rarely show coercion (which would undermine his previous argument), he insists that this means the women depicted appear as ever-ready to accommodate any sexual request from anybody in the vicinity. And that, worse, they are frequently shown taking the initiative in signalling their readiness! How does he know this, and why is this so bad anyway?

In other words, Zillmann is asserting that there is only one message contained in pornography, that there is only one interpretation of this message, and that this single message will be consumed by *all* readers of the material. It should go without saying that no communication theorist would agree with this simplistic model; it was abandoned 50 years ago (McQuail, 1987).

Suppose for a moment, however, that Zillmann were correct. Logic would dictate that the message of pornography is that *every* person can enjoy instrumental sexual activity. To ensure we do not reach this conclusion, however, Zillmann claims that pornography has a special message for men. The information that 'men are bound to extract' from pornography is that sexual satisfaction does not depend upon liking, loving or caring; that women are sexually insatiable and indiscriminate in sexual partner choice; and that women enjoy sexual 'rough housing' – all of which are self-serving male beliefs.

The reason this message is so dangerous for Zillmann is that pornography's alleged unique vividness and repetitiveness induces a degree of excitement that surpasses all other forms of information. The result, for men, is a disposition towards a belief in sexual entitlement.

The obvious difficulty with this suggestion is that Zillmann takes no account of female readers at all. More bizarre, however, is the claim that images 'must' increase in strength with repeated exposure, because in his most famous study, Zillmann has asserted that it is precisely the 'boredom' experienced with pornography that leads people to seek out other more violent and bizarre forms (Zillmann, 1989). Zillmann is using mutually exclusive arguments to support his claims of undesirable effects.

So what makes Zillmann so sure that he is correct? He claims 'considerable research support'. In reality, this amounts to Mohr and Zanna's discovery that males exposed to a pornographic film sat closer to a female research assistant and looked at her more than a control group did; Bernstein et al.'s discovery that removing the facial features of pornographic pictures did not reduce males' appreciation of the models' other attributes; Leonard and Taylor's experiment in which males recorded higher aggression levels against women who were sex-positive than those who were sex-negative; and Weaver's studies demonstrating that those exposed to explicit pornography gave rapists a lower sentence in a mock trial (Zillmann and Weaver, 1989).

With the best will in the world, these examples hardly constitute 'considerable' support, particularly when we could explain each and every finding in terms of Kelley's model, which demonstrated that it is men with conservative and stereotypical sexual attitudes who demonstrate aggressive and callous attitudes toward women. Even if we ignore Kelley's insights, other alternative explanations are easily offered: the males not exposed to pornography were embarrassed or inhibited by close contact; why should the absence of a face mean anything; Leonard and Taylor's experiment was very controversial as it involved a female confederate deliberately provoking retaliation. The last study requires greater consideration.

At first sight, demonstrating that those exposed to pornography tend to give mock trial defendants or media report rapists a lower sentence than control groups clearly supports the charge of callous induced behaviour. The charge is even more serious because the effect has been observed in experiments using soft-core material. These experiments, however, suffer from three major drawbacks that must be considered before one infers a direct link between soft-core consumption and the lower sentencing policy. First, these studies have proven difficult to replicate. Second, one would have to explain why, in some studies, hard-core exposure leads to higher sentencing, especially by those exhibiting hypermasculinity. Third, women often give lower sentences!

From a universalistic picture of a biological urge making men callous towards women, Zillmann has narrowed callousness to a tendency (in reality exhibited by only 23 per cent on his evidence) towards coercive sexual activity and subscription to a rape myth (in reality only directed towards some women), which emerges from male socialization and is directed by pornography towards women. Proof of pornography's seminal role in the process relies upon a belief that no other forms of socialization exist during teen years, and an extremely narrow appraisal of pornography's content. Behind these suggestions lie two absurd inferences: first, young men appear never to come into contact with women other than in pornography; and second, the sexist and patronizing assumption that women cannot engage in instrumental sexual activity outside a permanent loving relationship without being plied with drink or threatened with disengagement from the relationship. Women, apparently, can not enjoy sexual intercourse for its own sake, can never take the initiative, and would never seek to end emotional attachment. And yet he also tells us that women appear to be attracted to men who believe that women behave like this.

What this all boils down to is an assertion that sexual callousness would not exist without pornography – which is read by all consumers in the same way – because *all* men have this disposition, even though he can only find 23 per cent of them! Can we really trust a researcher with such confused and sexist reasoning?

8 Correlation Studies

The claim that there is a clear relationship between pornography consumption and rape rates ignores the 'fact' that a correlation merely demonstrates an association between two variables: it does not demonstrate 'cause.' Most social scientific studies using correlation only do so as an aid to further inquiry, not as the end point of a study. They also derive the correlation of the two variables chosen, such as pornography consumption and sex crime, as compared to other non-correlational variables. To say simply that a correlation exists is meaningless. Any serious correlational study would test numerous potential correlations (called regression analysis) on the data before making claims concerning 'possible' cause. Only one study of that kind exists: Baron and Strauss, 1986.

Before going on to review the pornography effects research, we must bear in mind the three major caveats discussed earlier:

1. The reliance of this research upon the Buss Paradigm fails to pay enough attention to the subjects' own interpretations and motivations. Researchers too quickly assume that the actions of the subjects are related to the variable researchers seek to test. Studies deliberately designed to test the effect of

experiment participation upon actions demonstrates how powerful the experiment process is.

2. As the review of one of Malamuth's major research papers demonstrates, accepted 'findings' can bear no relationship to the methodologies involved. In this case, the figures for likelihood to rape attitudes were secured only by manipulating both the questionnaire and the answers recorded.

3. As the review of Zillmann's theory on sex callousness demonstrates, aggression researchers' explanation of effects, and the concepts used in those explanations, rest upon dubious assertions. In this case, Zillmann's exposition of the existence of pornographically induced sexual callousness is a catalogue of assumptions and contradictory sexist beliefs.

Let us suppose, however, that such qualifications – regarding the methodology, validity, and casualty – do not exist. What does the pornography-aggression research tell us?

A Review of Pornography Effects Research

Sex Offenders

The fact that systematic research suggests that as many as one-third of American sex offenders utilized pornography directly prior to and/or during their crime (Marshall, 1989) continues to justify the search for the link. Some offenders may simply use pornography as an excuse; however, the major problem is that the figures are calculated from a false premise – the home-produced polaroids, frequently taken by child abuse offenders, are included in the study's figures. These materials cannot in any way be regarded as commercial pornography, and their exclusion from the studies drastically reduces the figures.

In any event, the fairly strong consensus among researchers is that sex offenders invariably had *less* exposure to pornography than the average male – a point accepted even by the Meese Commission (Walker, 1970; Cook et al., 1971; Kant and Goldstein, 1978; Meese Commission, 1986). Several studies have found that sex offenders appear to be more aroused by pornography showing the use of coercion by males on non-consenting females, when compared to control groups (Abel et al., 1977; Abel et al., 1978; Abel et al., 1981; Quinsey and Chaplin, 1984). But these findings are disputed (Baxter et al., 1986; Marshall et al., 1986). More intriguing, however, is that Wydra et al. (1983) found that rapists can control their arousal to exposure; therefore, we must wonder if we can trust any experiment that relies upon testing their arousal. Whether or not this is the case, no direct relationship between the consumption level of pornography and frequency of sex crime/degree of violence among offenders – a stronger test – has been found (Abel et al., 1985). Other researchers working in asylums for the criminally insane even argue that the sadistic rapist is more likely to be drawn to gory crime and detective magazines rather than to pornography (Groth and Hobson, 1983; Dietz et al., 1986).

There does, however, appear to be a relationship between family background and sex crimes: sex offenders tend to have grown up in households where there was almost no discussion of sexuality, but conformity to 'traditional' or 'conservative' sexual values was stressed in the form of proscriptions (Kant and Goldstein, 1978). There also appear to be higher correlations between family backgrounds of high alcohol consumption, violence, sexual abuse and sex crimes (Rada, 1978; Langevin et al., 1985). One study discovered that all rapists in the sample who had been found reading pornography in their teens were severely punished, while only 7 per cent of a cohort sample caught with this material were punished (Goldstein et al., 1973). Perhaps it's time we paid as much attention to sexual socialization as we do to pornography when it comes to influences upon sex offenders.

Soft-core Pornography

Almost every major researcher has found that soft-core pornography can *inhibit* aggression in individuals (Baron, 1974b; Baron and Bell, 1973, 1977; Donnerstein et al., 1975; White, 1979; Frodi, 1977; Zillmann and Sapolsky, 1977). Baron, for example, exposed two sets of viewers to either non-sexual pictures or those from *Playboy*. When the viewers were not angered beforehand, the group viewing *Playboy* demonstrated no effect on their aggression level. When angered, however, those viewing pornography demonstrated *lower* levels of aggression than the control group (Baron, 1974a).

Correlations

The belief that correlational studies have demonstrated links between pornography and sex crime rests upon the work of John Court, a Mary Whitehouse supporter. He has claimed that correlations exist not only between pornography and rape rates in various countries, but also between the rape rate and the content of the pornography available (Court, 1976, 1979, 1980a and b, 1981, 1982). Court, however, has never actually conducted a study as such. Selective reading of others' work has led him to suggest that:

1. countries that have liberalized their pornography laws have seen a corresponding rise in rape rates;
2. countries that have stricter controls against pornography have lower rape rates;
3. where pornography laws have become strict, such as in Japan, there has been a corresponding decrease in rape rates.

For each suggestion, however, obvious contradictions can be found. In Britain, sex offences have risen dramatically since strict limits were placed upon video film content and public displays of nudity (Thompson, 1987) and 500 sex shops were closed.

While Court's second suggestion may hold true for Singapore, on which he rests his case, in Stockholm – which next to Los Angeles has probably the highest pornography output in the world – there is a lower increase in rape rate than in Singapore, which has extremely severe sentences for conviction. Claims of this nature also fail to take into account the vast underground network of prostitution that exists in Singapore. The third observation fails to note the exact nature of the law involved. Japanese controls are strict, but the material is freely available in controlled outlets, and its content is some of the most 'violent' available: bondage, domination and torture make up the mainstream.

These examples not only demonstrate the weakness of attempts to establish simple correlations, but any global comparison runs the risk of ignoring other cultural features in the countries concerned. For example, no consideration was given to differences in the rate of reporting rape, and cultures still exist where women may fear social chastisement if they were to report a sexual assault. Propositions of this kind can not have universal applications.

Baron and Strauss once attempted a direct statistical correlation between soft-core consumption and rape rates in the USA (Baron and Strauss, 1984, 1985, 1986). While they did find a *per capita* correlation between the sales and rape rates, the correlation would be meaningless without a corresponding check on hard-core sales. When Scott did just that, he found no correlation at all (Scott, 1985).

In any event, there is no direct correlation in the Baron and Strauss study – Missouri has a higher rape rate *per capita* than Kansas, but Kansas sells almost twice as many soft-core magazines *per capita* than Missouri; Mississippi has the lowest *per capita* sales figures, but a rape rate higher than 17 other states! Indeed, when they tested regression analysis on a third variable, which they call the 'Violent Approval Index' (an intriguing 'hypermasculinity' check list) they found that males exhibiting this tendency were more likely to buy sex magazines and aggress against females, and found the simple correlation between soft-core sales and rape rates disappeared (Baron and Strauss, 1986)!

Scott also found a strong correlation between sales of country sports magazines in the various states and rape rates. More work is clearly needed in this area.

Explicit Pornography and Male Aggression

Early studies like Mosher's found an increase in 'aggression' using verbal abuse as the test, and the researcher also 'rewarded' offenders by allowing them to view another erotic film if males were rude to women (Mosher, 1970)! Studies like Baron's which did not pre-anger subjects demonstrated a decrease in aggression (Baron et al., 1973a and b, and 1974).

To explain this apparent contradiction, Donnerstein developed a theory known as the 'arousal shift' theory. He argued that those studies which had found aggression tended to be those using explicit pornographic films showing intercourse, while those studies finding no effect tended to be those using non-explicit pornographic magazines.

He tested his thesis during the 1970s by checking how arousing the material was. When different types of magazine photographs were shown to three groups, there was no increase in aggression whatever the content. When angered, the subjects exposed to pin-up imagery demonstrated *lower* aggression, and those exposed to explicit material exhibited no increase in aggression. In other words, explicit pornography did not increase aggression, and soft-core decreases aggression levels (Donnerstein et al., 1975).

Surprised at these results, Donnerstein tried again but this time altered the levels of anger and arousal in subjects. Males provoked by females or male confederates before exposure to extremely explicit material were more physiologically aroused and did demonstrate more aggression than a control group; but there was no difference in recorded aggression levels against male and female confederates (Donnerstein and Barrett, 1978).

Failing to find the result he expected, and determined to prove men should demonstrate higher levels of aggression against women, Donnerstein encouraged just that by ensuring subjects observed another male aggressing against a female before their own test. The results backfired; despite being angered by a female confederate and shown very explicit films, when very physiologically aroused the group recorded a higher level of aggression against male confederates, not against the women! In plain English, despite being encouraged to aggress against women, men exposed to very heavy pornography did not do so (Donnerstein and Hallam, 1978).

To sum up: experiments in the 1970s had demonstrated that soft core reduced aggression levels, and that hard core, while provoking increased levels of aggression, did not direct it specifically against women. This clearly suggested arousal rates followed the experiment, not the content. So where does the belief that pornography provokes violence come from?

We first find it in a 1978 experiment conducted by Donnerstein and Hallam who deliberately encouraged those who did not show aggression to have another go! Likewise, when Leonard and Taylor attempted to replicate the study five years later, males aggressed against the female confederate only after she had continually made comments which implied she wished to act out the scenes in the pornography viewed, but at the same time contemptuously gave the male subjects higher and higher levels of electric shock (Leonard and Taylor, 1983). Not only could this be seen as an act of retaliation, but no credit appears to have been given to the subjects who long delayed a retaliatory aggressive act under conditions amounting to torture.

In the meantime, Zillmann had discovered the rationale for all laboratory aggressive acts. In a series of experiments, he realized that the subjects' actions are only partly determined by their anger; arousal does not follow the level of explicitness so much as whether or not they approve of the content. If they found the material pleasing, the level of aggression would fall; but if the subject found the material displeasing or revolting, the level of aggression would increase. The material producing the greatest amount of aggression? An explicit film about an eye operation (Zillmann et al., 1981).

These findings should have stunned the research community. They meant that pornography study subjects' aggression levels had less to do with the sexual content or even with the themes displayed than with the subjects' reaction to it. The highest levels of aggression would come from those finding the material objectionable! Yet only Kelley, from New York State University, began to explore the relationship between prior sexual attitudes and sexual fantasy provoked by viewing various forms of pornography, and confirmed that effects were dependent on the subjects' sexual attitudes rather than on the content of the material they were exposed to. When Kelley tested a group's reaction to four films differing in the level of aggressive content, male subjects who had 'positive' sexual attitudes demonstrated the least anti-social effects. The most important feature appeared to be the role of 'sex-guilt' feelings (Kelley, 1985).

The implications of this research on other studies, which did not seek the subjects' attitude towards sexuality prior to the tests, are obvious.

In a second study, Kelley and Musialowski tested the relationship between attitudes towards censorship and violent sexual stimulus. Those subjects with 'negative' sexual attitudes were far more likely to recommend censorship, and the female subjects involved were more likely to develop negative attitudes towards males following exposure (Kelley and Musialowski, 1986).

Unfortunately, the clear inference that adverse sexual socialization may be the root cause of aggression demonstrated after viewing pornography, and that this needs to be explained, was not seen as a fit line of inquiry by the rest of the research community. The same applies to a promising set of studies involving women's attitudes to pornography.

Conservatives have long argued that men and women have different innate attitudes and exhibit different reactions to pornography, and that women are less aggressive than men. Cultural feminists promote a similar idea, and both groups argue that pornography promotes a single stereotype of women which is degrading, and that women are adversely affected by this single message (Thompson and Annetts, 1990).

In 1979 Baron published results of standard effects test where women were substituted for men, angered by a female researcher in the usual manner, and then exposed to varieties of photographs to induce different levels of arousal. When given the opportunity to aggress against the confederate, those viewing bathing-suited males demonstrated reduced aggression levels; those viewing soft core demonstrated no change in aggressive levels either way; those viewing copulating couples demonstrated increased aggression. Women who were not aggressed by the researcher before viewing demonstrated no aggression, irrespective of the stimuli (Baron, 1979). Other research projects discovered similar results (Jaffe et al., 1974; Fisher and Harris, 1976; Cantor et al., 1978). It is difficult to determine what we make of these results: do they demonstrate the same 'reaction' as males – i.e. that increased arousal can increase the possibility of aggression – or were the results related to the subjects' level of disgust invoking greater arousal and hence aggression?

It's an intriguing question, especially when Krafka discovered that female subjects viewing pornography that was deemed de-humanizing and degrading by the researchers did *not* report greater sex-role stereotyping, lower self-esteem, or inferiority regarding their looks (Krafka, 1985). In contrast, Cash found women had lower self-esteem after viewing pictures of models in mainstream magazine advertisements (Cash et al., 1983, quoted in Donnerstein et al., 1987).

Clearly, women have a similar arousal and aggression response to men, but not a lower soft-core aggression level. As to the belief that pornography provokes adverse feelings regarding self-image, this was not the case. This unanswered question was to become central in later studies.

Long-term Exposure to Explicit Material

The obvious problem with the studies in the 1970s was that they tested only short-term reactions. Zillmann and Bryant correctly argued that long-term studies were required to test the material's real effects. By exposing three subject groups over a six-week period to three different forms of material – neutral films, a mix of neutral and sexual films, and sexual films – they hoped to provide a more meaningful result.

The outcome? Those exposed to sexual films exhibited *less* aggression than those exposed to the neutral films! The mixed group demonstrated a slight decrease in aggression. The results were the same for both females and males.

The implications did not stop there. This repeated exposure drastically reduced the viewers' physiological arousal and subjects' negative feelings towards content. As aggression depends upon physiological arousal, Zillmann was faced with the embarrassing conclusion that the more you watch pornography, the less likely you are to be provoked by the material (Zillmann and Bryant, 1989). So why does pornography appear to lead to violent acts by some people? Part of the answer may be found in the mid-1980s studies testing reactions to violent, as opposed to explicit, material.

This research was justified by the claim that pornography *per se* was becoming more violent, itself a dubious assumption (Palys, 1986; Thompson and Annetts, 1990). But the research found this was not the issue, either. As far back as 1978 Malamuth had found subjects exposed to 'rape' stories – in which the woman 'enjoyed' the experience – produced a higher level of aggression (compared to those exposed to a non-aggressive sexual scenario, and a control group) when encouraged to aggress, after being angered by the target (Malamuth, 1978). Studies by Donnerstein produced similar results. Whereas highly explicit films produced no increase in aggression in angered subjects, 'rape-myth' films did so in non-angered subjects, as long as the victim was shown to enjoy the experience (Donnerstein and Berkowitz, 1981). These apparently clear-cut cases were, however, challenged by a contemporaneous longitudinal study by Malamuth and Ceniti who found no difference between the levels of aggression in subjects watching violent material, non-violent explicit material, and a control group (Malamuth and Ceniti, 1986). On the other hand, further studies suggested that even if viewers did not become more aggressive, their attitudes towards women with regard to rape victims' culpability changed (Malamuth et al., 1980). But while subjects exposed to a rape story in which the woman displayed pleasure assigned less suffering to a woman in a second story of 'non-pleasurable' rape, these same subjects, when asked to assign a mock trial sentence, recorded the heaviest given in the study! In other words, the subjects' attitudes towards the victim did not translate into a favourable attitude towards rapists. When the subjects were differentiated by their high likelihood to rape score, only those exhibiting a high score revealed an increase in the belief that women enjoy rape and engaging in forced sex (Malamuth and Check, 1985).

Faced with these findings, it began to dawn upon Donnerstein and others that the effect of violent pornography was not found in engendering callous attitudes, but reinforcing prior attitudes. Both he and Malamuth then changed their research direction; unfortunately they still did not check Kelley's implications that those holding conservative and traditional values became aggressive. As the results clearly imply that males who have adverse attitudes to women enjoy watching films which they perceive prove that women can not resist a macho man's advances, this should have been obvious.

Malamuth and Check had already begun to explore the effects of non-explicit sexually orientated violence on subjects at the beginning of the decade. They argued that general release films like *The Getaway* and *Swept Away* increased subjects' acceptance of rape myths. Such interpretations were debatable (see Tong, 1989, pp. 117). Be that as it may, Donnerstein now tried to differentiate the sex from the violence, and found that 'aggression only' films produced greater increases in aggression than highly explicit non-violent films (Donnerstein et al., 1986). A second study using a 'rape-myth acceptance' scale, similar to HLR scales, found that the most callous attitudes emerged from the 'aggression only' film exposure subjects, and that subjects exposed to the 'explicit sex only' film recorded the lowest scores. The message was clear: explicit sex does not encourage negative attitudes towards women, but callous people are aroused by violent movies (especially those showing knife-wielding psychos stalking bimbo freshers dressed in their underwear). Malamuth produced similar results (Malamuth et al., 1986).

As a result, Donnerstein became convinced that focusing research on sexually explicit violent imagery ignored the more serious problem of aggression against women in 'R' rated (i.e. slasher-type) movies which did not contain sexually explicit scenes (Donnerstein et al., 1987). These findings, however, were rigorously challenged by Fisher and Grenier who, when replicating studies, found that violent material did *not* produce any difference in attitudes towards women, acceptance of violence, 'rape myths' and so on (Fisher and Grenier, 1988). If we are to draw a conclusion, it has to be that Kelley's hypothesis regarding prior attitudes demands more attention.

Exploring Violence

Adding Donnerstein's observations to Zillmann's results blows a big hole in the anti-pornography crusaders' desensitization thesis; if constant exposure does desensitize people, how can it simultaneously provide the physiological arousal required to turn anger into physical aggression? It can not.

The real issue is why exposure to sexually explicit violence produces different results in different people. The obvious area to explore is the subjects' prior attitudes and proclivities, which lead them to interpret the scenes they see in a particular way. More importantly, we have to find out why it is that even non-callous desensitized viewers sometimes perceive rape victims as less harmed, and give lower sentences to rapists in mock studies (Donnerstein et al.,1987). Some tentative answers are provided by the growing number of studies that began to concentrate upon violence.

When Linz conducted his experiments he screened subjects for high psychoticism, i.e. people who exhibit little empathy with others, a predisposition to violence, very instrumental sexual desires, and numerous other anti-social traits, including highly adverse attitudes towards women. By removing those with such tendencies from the group, he could argue prior adverse attitudes would not cause the reaction to the content of five 'R' rated movies: *Texas Chainsaw Massacre, Maniac, I Spit on Your Grave, Vice Squad* and *Toolbox Murders*. These 'normal' viewers steadily rated the films as less violent irrespective of the order in which the films were shown to them (Linz et al., 1984; Linz, 1985). Despite being desensitized, however, they also reported seeing more examples of scenes designated as a sexual assault upon, or rape of, women; i.e. they became more sensitized to sexual violence! Yet they still saw a mock rape trial defendant as less responsible for the alleged crime than a control group. What is going on?

Part of the confusion is caused by methodological assumptions. First, subjects' simulated rape trial results are not compared with a comparative simulation involving violence against men; thus, the inference drawn that men become 'callous' towards women *per se* – because they did not empathize totally with the simulation rape victim – is only conjecture. Second, it should be noted that when female subjects are used, they not only become equally 'desensitized', they are even more reluctant to sympathize with the victim – effectively scoring a greater degree of 'male callousness' toward women than men do (Zillmann, 1989)! Numerous sexist suggestions have been put forward to explain this observation, none of which take account of the methodology; typical is Donnerstein's belief that the women steeled themselves against the impression that they could not control negative events (Donnerstein et al., 1987). Such explanations enable these researchers to avoid facing the obvious implication that their initial hypothesis may require modification, and that their methodology does not allow us to uncover what is going on in the minds of the subjects.

Thompson has begun to explore an alternative possibility. He argues that the 'R' movie viewers may impose situational reasoning upon content, such as assessing culpability, and that subjects do not utilize ideologically absolute standards. Such a conclusion was supported by his and Amendolia's 1991 date-rape study (Thompson et al., 1990; Amendolia and Thompson, 1991). Thompson points out that many 'R' films promote the prurient 'message' that the victims 'deserve' retribution for breaking a moral taboo against sound advice, and because they have foolishly placed themselves in further danger by ignoring all reason. A typical plot, for example, would show drunken teenagers holding a sex orgy in a former monastery, then 'splitting up' to find a colleague who has wandered off and has been missing for hours, despite knowing the mad axe murderer is on the warpath. 'R' movies can, therefore, be seen as morality tales, warning viewers against the potential dangers of permissiveness and stupidity (Thompson and Annetts, 1990). Many of the reduced scores recorded by both women and men could, therefore, be explained by this 'sensitization' to stupidity. This might help explain the verdicts regarding culpability in the rape trial simulations, and the female subjects' belief that they are less likely to be a victim. If this is the case, the clinical researchers have failed to notice that 'R' rated movies present a qualitatively different message from pornography, and that this prevents a direct comparison with study results obtained from exposure to pornography. In 'R' movies, the victims are shown as 'deserving' their fate; in pornography this interpretation may often require a sex callous predisposition.

Either way, when testing British University students' attitudes to date rapists and their victims, Amendolia and Thompson found that these likely viewers of 'R' movies did not utilize ideologically absolute standards of culpability, but applied a situational one relating both to the amount of force and deviousness of the male, and the 'foolishness' exhibited by the female, so that while rapists were always held to be ultimately responsible, the victim was also perceived as culpable to varying extents. While the ideologically correct may not approve of this attitude, it exists, and needs to be accounted for when assessing reasons for lower sentencing in mock rape trials. We need to check exactly what scenarios were provided in the tests conducted by clinical researchers to see if such a factor may have been at work, and why researchers did not bother to ask their subjects why they recorded lower scores for the rapists. At the very least, those researching in this area need to differentiate between the scenarios offered in their trial simulations.

Callousness Explored

Being less inclined to absolve pornography, Zillmann and Bryant took a different path, and continued to search for a link between soft core and sex aggression by exploring divisions between different forms of non-violent material. In their oft-quoted 'massive exposure' studies of material deemed 'demeaning and debasing' to women (defined by such scenes as a male ejaculating upon a female face), both male and female subjects appear to have become: more tolerant to what researchers labelled 'bizarre and violent' pornography; less supportive of statements deemed to be supporting 'sexual equality'; and more lenient in assigning mock trial rapists punishment (Zillmann and Bryant, 1982 and 1984). Zillmann, therefore, concluded that demeaning soft core clearly increased 'sexual callousness towards women'. Those feminists who concur and quote these studies gloss over four problems, apart from the failure to determine what the subjects' interpretation of the material was.

First, many of the effects accredited to these massive exposure experiments actually come from later studies (Zillmann and Bryant, 1986, 1988 and 1989); the popularizers can not even quote the correct studies.

Second, throughout all these studies, Zillmann and Bryant's definition of adverse effects is extremely sexist and conservative. Just look at some of the attitudes reported that they deem 'adverse': believing having several partners is more natural than life-long monogamy; believing there is nothing wrong with pre- and extra-marital sexual activities; not believing marriage is an essential institution; expressing less desire to have children; and being more likely to believe that repressing sexual desire is unhealthy! To say that pornography has an adverse effect because those exposed to it were more likely to articulate such attitudes is a value judgement; what is wrong with holding such beliefs? The same applies to what the authors saw as the most dramatic attitudinal change. Whereas almost half of the control group believed 'promiscuity' was acceptable for men but not for women, those exposed to pornography did not share this hypocrisy. The real question to ask, therefore, is why do feminists quote research so clearly based upon the value judgements of a social conservative like Zillmann?

Third, the study revealing the most dramatic changes in attitude is invalid anyway. When the study's groups were separated into controls and those going to watch the pornography, the older, more conservative-minded subjects in the exposure group withdrew, refusing to watch the material and thereby leaving the younger, more 'liberal' subjects, upon which Zillmann's claims to attitudinal change were made. Those remaining in the control group may well have exhibited the beliefs recorded before exposure to the material, anyway. To compare such a group with the same control group would almost certainly have produced such results. Zillmann, himself, has admitted as much.

> The withdrawal rate upon revelation of the nature of the research was substantial ... As a result, the findings on non-students cannot be considered representative ... (Zillmann, 1989, p. 139)

Therefore, the negative answers given by subjects to a Value of Marriage Survey and the Indiana Inventory of Personal Happiness questionnaires were inevitable.

Fourth, these supposedly 'adverse' effects were complemented by a marked *decrease* in those same subjects' aggressive behaviour.

The problem with all these 'callous' attitude studies is that they made no attempt to check pre-exposure attitudes for sex negatives along the lines of Kelley's model, HLR proclivities following Malamuth's model, or psychoticism – studies which do provide very interesting results. When Check recorded subjects' reactions following different levels of exposure to violent, dehumanizing (Zillmann's 'demeaning'), and erotic soft core, having pre-tested for psychoticism, he found a clear link between psychoticism, exposure, age, and the subjects' scores on numerous tests for propensity to rape, and propensities to use force (knowing they would not be punished). Check concluded:

> exposure to non-violent erotic materials did not have any demonstrated antisocial impact on any of the other independent variables. This was in contrast to sexually violent and dehumanizing material. (Check, 1985)

Once again, soft-core was given a clean bill of health and the role of prior attitude exposed as vital. Subjects exhibiting high psychoticism were twice as likely as the control group to report a potential to engage in rape and forceful acts after exposure. There were also two other interesting results.

The study sample deliberately included non-students. As a result, when students and non-students were compared, Check found that students exhibited a higher level of psychoticism and potential to rape than the public, which may well explain why previous studies relying upon students can not be applied to general populations.

Even more intriguing was that those exposed to violent material who had low psychoticism scores were less likely to report a potential to rape than all the other groups involved – be they controls, soft-core viewers or 'dehumanizing' viewers. If we accept the premises upon which the other findings were based, this would mean that violent pornography reduces aggression in low psychoticism subjects!

Whatever the reason for this observed effect, this study provoked a debate regarding Check's use of material, and Zillmann's findings regarding 'soft-core' material.

The major contention was whether the 'dehumanizing' scenes extracted from numerous films out of context, to make up tapes for the subjects, effectively altered the effect of the whole film and any implied motivation in real life. When Linz tested this criticism by showing complete films such as *Debbie Does Dallas* to replicate Check's extracts, viewers' scores on callous attitude, sexism, rapist's non-culpability, and rape victim's culpability did not increase (Linz, 1985). Similar studies by Krafka (1985), and Malamuth and Ceniti produced the same result (Malamuth and Ceniti, 1986).

But such a dispute highlights doubts about the labelling of films' content by the researchers, and the problem of decontextualized film extracts from various genres. Are the demeaning scenes really demeaning? Were these scenes 'seen' as demeaning by the subjects? If they were 'seen' as demeaning, we do not know whether the subjects' reaction is related to the context of the whole film in which they are seen. A study by Weaver attempted to clarify the position using four different categories of film extract – explicit lovers, nymphomania (sic) behaviour, rape, and non-sexual threats against women – and tested the subjects' sentencing policy in two mock rape cases. Although the exposure had no differential effect on subjects' assessments of a case involving a male assault on a female cohabitant, the subjects exposed to the nymphomania (sic) extracts passed much lower sentences in a 'stranger' rape case; as much as 37 per cent lower than controls – the exact opposite of previous experiments that would have led us to expect such a result after the rape movie (Weaver, 1987).

While this confirms Thompson's suggestion that the nature of the offences in the trials affects outcome as much as content, we clearly need more experiments in this area.

Conclusion

While anti-pornography activists are correct in their assertion that contemporary aggression studies come to different conclusions than those of the past, the findings are not what they imply.

Time and time again, soft-core pornography far more explicit than that available in Britain has been shown to lower aggression levels. Convicted rapists who allege pornography led them to commit their crime do not appear to utilize this form of pornography. Correlational studies do not demonstrate a clear relationship between soft-core pornography consumption and rape rates. Violent material of a non-sexually explicit nature does encourage aggression in pre-angered subjects. The reason for this appears to be related to the subjects' general sexual attitudes and socialization which induce 'sexual guilt' when viewing such material. Studies concerning rape-myth material are ambiguous and confusing. The researchers involved cannot agree among themselves why they obtain the results they do.

Studies that draw attention to sex callousness induced by pornography, even allowing for the manipulation of the content's meaning, have yet to explain why women appear to be more callous than men. The bizarre anomaly whereby liberal-minded students appear to record lower sentences in mock trials needs to be explored. Thompson has offered us one explanation, and this needs to be tested, and others explored.

Long-term exposure to pornography, however, appears to reduce the subjects' arousal, and thereby potential to aggress.

It is clear that many more factors than pornography content are involved, and that these need to be studied in order to explain laboratory aggression against women. It is possible that a person's beliefs and socialization are far more important than pornography when trying to determine why they commit sex crimes. And this raises an important question regarding our response to almost three decades of study. If we ignore the caveats that raise serious doubts concerning their scientific validity, and take the studies at face value, we need to ask why, after all this time, the studies still concentrate on the material rather than on the interrelationship between prior attitudes and effects.

It is quite clear that exposure to pornography encourages adverse reactions in those whose socialization mirrors the conservative anti-pornography crusaders' ideal. The fact that some feminists choose to ignore this implication in their obsession to eradicate all 'pornography' raises questions about their motivation. It surely is no accident that neither conservative nor anti-porn feminist reviews of the studies ever mention Kelley – the only woman working in this field – who demonstrated the importance of prior attitudes. Feminists should pay more attention to her work, with its implications regarding conservative patriarchal male attitudes.

Those of a more liberal persuasion, however, cannot afford to be smug. Whatever the shortcomings of these studies, and the nonsense written about callousness, the reason why women as well as men appear to demonstrate more lenient sentencing policies towards rapists needs to be explored. Thompson has offered one circumstantial reason for some studies; we need to explore others.

6

Essentially Sex: a New Look

ALISON ASSITER

In certain fashionable branches of contemporary philosophy and feminist theory, the predilection for 'constructivism' is being overtaken by an interest in 'essentialism'. Until very recently, to be tarred with the essentialist brush was to have committed a cardinal sin. In the last few years, however, feminists have begun to unravel the variety of meanings of the term, and, in some cases, even to valorize the concept. Diane Fuss, for example, argues that there are essentialist elements in the thought of those who, like Lacan, have been regarded as anti-essentialist. Additionally, some have argued that an essentialist stance is politically useful for groupings who have been regarded as 'others' in relation to a dominant group.[1] There is one area of critical discussion, however, where constructivist approaches have largely gone unquestioned: theories of sexuality. Constructivists about sexuality, I will argue, tend to deny the agency of sex workers, on the one hand, and rapists, on the other.

Biological Determinisms

Constructivists about sexuality were motivated by several interlocking concerns. One fear was the spectre of biological determination. This took on varying forms depending on the vantage point of the writer. One of the earliest types of 'biological determination' to which constructivists objected sees sexuality as a 'drive-based sexologic'.[2] The best-known exponents of this kind of view about sexuality were Wilhelm Reich and Freud. For Reich, sexuality is a universal biological drive, 'energy' that seeks satisfactory release. 'Neurotic' people, for Reich, ultimately suffer from sexual frustration. Reich contrasted neurotic people with those with 'genital characters' who possessed 'orgasmic potency'. This is 'the capacity for surrender to the flow of energy in the orgasm without any inhibitions; the capacity for complete discharge of all dammed-up sexual excitation through involuntary pleasurable contractions ... free of anxiety and unpleasure and unaccompanied by fantasies'.[3]

Freud sometimes assimilates sexual wishes or desires to biological drives that simply 'seek release'. He begins *The Three Essays on Sexuality*, for example, as follows: 'The fact of the existence of sexual needs in human beings and animals is expressed in biology by the assumption of a "sexual instinct", on the analogy of the instinct of nutrition'.[4] In another passage, he says:

> Popular opinion has quite definite ideas about the nature and characteristics of the sexual instinct. It is generally understood to be absent in childhood, to set in at the time of puberty in connection with the process of coming to maturity and to be revealed in the manifestations of an irresistible attraction exercised by one sex upon the other, while its aim is presumed to be sexual union ...[5]

The metaphor of the 'hydraulic model' is often used to describe Freud's view of sex drives – there is, for Freud, a constant supply of the 'sexual substance' that flows out through the mouth, the anus, the sex 'organs' and, on some readings of Freud, almost any other part of the body. Kinsey, too, emphasized the notion of a sexual 'outlet'.

One aspect of the constructivists' critique of such views is an objection to the language – sexual desire is not 'energy' or 'drives', it is not 'released' through 'outlets'. But additionally, constructivists have argued, the very language of 'energy' and 'drives' suggests its 'constructed' character. The language, it is perhaps interesting to note, contains a combination of metaphors from the science of hydraulics – sexuality is like water flowing through pipes, from the theory in physics of the constancy of the supply of energy, and from stimulus response theory in psychology/biology. No theory – biological or physical – in other words, is socially unconstructed or 'natural'. Rather, such theories often serve political and ideological functions. One biological theory that was commonplace in Victorian times was the view that human bodies in general contained a finite supply of energy. This theory was deployed to make the famous, highly political, claim that women should not be educated, since energy used up in such a domain detracts from the 'proper' application of energy for women in child-bearing and child-rearing.[6]

More important than criticizing the biological determinists' language as a metaphor, however, constructivists have objected that the metaphors are thought to be taken too literally. The Victorian writers above believed in the literal truth of the claim that the human body is a kind of receptacle, containing a finite amount of energy, some of which is sexual. Constructivists have claimed that this picture of sexuality does not ring true. Sexual desires are not like drives or energy seeking release; rather, they are only given meaning in social and cultural settings. There are two parts to this claim of the sexual constructivists: one is that any one sexual desire, expressed in a behavioural form – for example, kissing – takes on a different meaning depending on whether you are Roman, Barbarian, ancient Greek or contemporary Asian,[7] the other is that theorists like Reich, Freud (sometimes) and Kinsey attempt to reduce *any* psychical, social, linguistic or cultural aspects of sexuality to a biological 'essence'. One part of the critique, then, is that any one behavioural manifestation of a sexual desire takes on a variety of forms and meanings; the other is that biological determinists set out (wrongly) to reduce the desire to some biological essence.

Another aspect of biological determinist theory to which some constructivists have objected is this: drive-based sexuality, even if it is not all there is assumed to be to sexuality, is somehow seen to be 'foundational' to any other form. Sexuality, on this version of the biological determinist viewpoint, may not be wholly to do with drives or 'outlets', but these drives are real, rather like Lockean real essences, while their counterparts – desires and wishes – are only the logical and causal effects of these 'outlets' and are somehow, therefore, less 'real'. A constructivist of a sort, like Lacan, for example, analyses sexual drives through the mediation of language and linguistic processes. Sexual 'drives' are not real, biologically determined or natural; rather, they are mediated by the particular socio-cultural setting in which they present themselves. This socio-cultural setting, clearly, is variable.

There is a further part to certain constructivists' rejection of 'biology'. This is a reaction against what they see as the constructivist over-reliance on the 'science' of biology in the study of matters sexual. Jeffrey Weeks, for example, traces the faith of many sexologists that, in the struggle between sexual ignorance and enlightenment, biological and medical science would be the strongest weapon. He cites the case of Magnus Hirschfeld – a German sexologist – who saw his Berlin Institute seized and its papers burned by the Nazis, and yet who still proclaimed:

I believe in science, and I am convinced that science, and above all the human sciences, must bring to mankind, not only truth, but with Truth, Justice, Liberty and Peace.[8]

The study of sexual biology – instincts, brain centres, hormones, germ plasm, genes and more recently, vaginal blood flow and clitoral histochemistry – would, so ran the belief, provide nature's direction for human sexual conduct. Science would dictate the true nature of human sexuality.

Clearly, the Nazis thought differently about 'pure' objective science. They shared the social constructivist view that sexualities are 'constructed' by scientific discourses as they are by religious and psychoanalytic languages.

In this case, medical science was not a strong weapon in favour of sexual liberation; indeed, its fruits were destroyed in one fell swoop. An over-reliance on science, in attempting to create an emancipatory discourse on sexuality, then, may be appropriate. But, additionally, Weeks argues that to focus on sexual desire and sexual pleasure as measurable states is to paint a picture that is both inaccurate and potentially mystifacatory of the social and psychological aspects of sexuality. Again, here, it is the reductionist aspects of the physiological approach to sexuality that the constructivists describe as misleading.

There is a further aspect of the critique of biological determinism which emerges from recent feminist constructivist writing about sexuality. Several lesbian feminist writers have described the commitment, for example in psychoanalytic writing, to 'the institution of heterosexuality' (Sheila Jeffreys) as a form of biological determinism. For Monique Wittig, psychoanalysis assumes heterosexuality to be a natural phenomenon akin to a biological *apriora*. For her:

> there is no sex. There is but sex that is oppressed and sex that oppresses. It is oppression that creates sex and not the contrary. The contrary would be to say that sex creates oppression or to say that the cause (origin) of oppression is to be found in sex itself , in a natural division of the sexes pre-existing (or outside of) society.[9]

Any psychoanalytic theory, in other words, that purports to explain the production of self-identity and gendered difference is a type of biological determinist view, in so far as it presupposes a heterosexual mandate. Instead, Wittig advocates the abolition of the category of women and correspondingly new categories of person as materially oppressed grouping(s), and the production of a new epistemology that will replace forms of knowing that are dependent upon heterosexism. More recently, Butler has presented a version of Wittig's view.[10]

For Sheila Jeffreys, too, 'the institution of heterosexuality' functions effectively in a biological determinist fashion. She would not put it quite like this; rather, she describes it as a 'political institution'[11] created and sustained by a number of disparate discourses; for example, that of the sexologists at one extreme, the Marriage Guidance Council in post-war Britain and selected 1960s sexual revolutionaries at another. However, the effect, according to her, of these discourses, is to create heterosexuality as a biological given. True feminists, for her, must therefore actively choose to transcend their biology; they must (if necessary) refuse their desires and make the political choice of lesbianism.

The objections of these two constructivists – Wittig and Jeffreys – to the form of biological determinism in question here is akin to the aforementioned difficulties with the more general type of biological determinism. Either desire is effectively reduced to heterosexual desire, or the latter is foundational for any other type of desire. The idea of a foundation, anyway, constructivists argue, is misleading in so far as no biological phenomenon can be described in terms that make no reference to social or experiential terms.

Extending this, there is a further type of contructivism. Some feminists recently have expressed considerable interest in 'the body and its desires' (see E. Grosz and S. Bordo, for example). They would argue, however, that no aspect of a person's make-up – her instincts, desires and wishes through to her beliefs – can be regarded as immune from social and cultural conditioning. These feminists would not so much reject biology as argue that its content is socially constructed. This type of constructivism, indeed, is present in Foucault.

Constructivisms: a Critique

One form of constructivism about sexuality is the view that one's sexuality is a matter of conscious political choice; Sheila Jeffreys, for example, argues that we can make a conscious choice to give up a particular sexual identity, preference for sexual object or set of sexual desires. A more common approach of sexual constructivists, however, is to see both sexual identity and sexual desire as 'a product of social and historical forces'.[12] Sexuality, for Weeks, is a 'fictional unity' that once did not exist and at some time in the future may not exist again. Weeks is critical of the 'essentialist' approach to sex, and argues that existing languages of sex set the horizon of the possible; there are, he argues, vast ranges and types of sexualities and no certainties about the matter.

Weeks has done an enormous amount of historical research in support of his position. He demonstrates the multiplicity of sexualities, from variations in the form taken by the kinship taboo – 'in the Christian traditions of the Middle Ages', for example, 'marriage to the 7th degree of relationships was prohibited ...[13] In the Egypt of the Pharaohs, sibling marriages were permitted' to the varying patterns of family life. He quotes Freud: 'The most striking difference between the erotic life of antiquity and our own no doubt lies in the fact that the ancients laid the stress upon the instinct itself, whereas we emphasise its object.'

Perhaps the prime progenitor, for many, of recent sexual constructivisms, is Foucault. Sex and sexualities are, for him, the forms of one of the knowledge–power couplets; sexualities proliferated from the seventeenth century on as discourses – Catholicism, medicine, psychiatry, etc. Discourses of sexuality might take on the character of, for instance, 'the internal discourse of the 18th century school' – its architectural layout, the rules for monitoring bedtime and sleep periods, the planning of the recreation lessons, or more obvious forms, like the speech of educators, physicians, parents, about, for instance, children's sex.[14] But whatever the form they have taken, discourses on sexuality have flourished. Sex, Foucault says, 'became transformed into discourse'.

The discourses of sexuality, according to common readings of Foucault, are one particularly crucial set of exemplifications of the 'regimes of truth' that he seeks to unmask. Medicine, for example, purports to reveal 'the truth' about people's sexualities. In fact, Foucault argues, this commitment to 'the truth' is itself the crucial manifestation of power. The 'science' of medicine creates forms of oppression – the 'pervert', the pederast. The discourses on sexuality construct the subject of sexual desire; 'The subject is not the vis-a-vis of power but one of its prime effects.'[15] A person's constitution as a subject is inseparable from her subjection to the power of a 'great interpreter' who is assumed to have privileged access to the truth. In the Catholic confessional, for example, the individual – via the mediation of the priest ('the interpreter') – constructs himself/herself as a sexed being. The sexed subject, then, is subjugated in two senses: in the sense that she/he is 'subject to another by control' and in that she is 'tied to her own identity by consequence of self-knowledge'.

As many commentators have pointed out, Foucault is less interested in revealing some fundamental truth about heterosexual behaviour than in describing how the subject is constructed and controlled through the multifarious discourses on sexuality. For example, demography serves the scientific purpose of achieving population control; psychology, sexology, psychoanalysis – the key 'modern' discourses on sexuality – each seeks to locate some fundamental truth about the individual as revealed in her/his sexual behaviour.

Another constructivist of a sort, Lacan[16] analyses sexual drives as mediated through language and linguistic processes. Sexual drives are not 'real', biologically determined or natural; rather, they are functions of the effect of the field of the other. The biological 'stages' in the development of sexuality, described by Freud, must be understood, for Lacan, to be mediated by the particular socio-cultural settings in which the child finds him/herself.

Of course, there are vast differences between these various 'constructivisms'. However, most of them, I would argue, have down-played the role of the biological in sexuality. Foucault, Lacan and, latterly, J. Weeks and others, have sought to provide an antidote, particularly to the work of the sexologists. These people were setting out, for the first time, to categorize and identify forms of sexual practice and sexual desire that had previously not been recognized. Weeks has pointed to the work of the eighteenth-century writer Tissot, who warned of the dangers of masturbation. Tissot's work, he argues, marked a transition from a view of this activity as infringing divine law to its helping determine what sort of person you are.[17] In the 1860s and 1870s, Karl Heinrich Ulrichs published twelve volumes on homosexuality (which was given its name by Berkert in 1869).[18] This pioneering work marked the way for Kraft-Ebbing's writings on the 'sexual aberrations'.

The nineteenth-century writers were seeking to identify what they saw as 'natural' processes or instincts. As many writers have argued, their work must be seen in the context of Darwin's claim (in *The Descent of Man* and *Selection in Relation to Sex*) that sexual selection acted independently from natural selection so that survival depended on sexual selection. This work led to an interest in the sexual 'origins' of behaviour and particular concern with sexual impulses and the differences between the sexes.

The nineteenth-century sexologists, following Darwin, argued that there was a natural process underlying individual experiences.

Certain constructivists, drawing on the 'non-biologistic' aspects of Freud's writings and on the work of early sociologists like Goffman, have stressed that sexuality is about two things: choice, for some of them, and social processes, for others.

There is no question that the assumption of the label 'homosexual' is partly a matter of choice. Sexologists, since Kinsey, have pointed out that there is no necessary connection between sexual behaviour and sexual identity. Kinsey documented the fact that 37 per cent of men had homosexual experiences to orgasm, yet only 4 per cent of men assumed the identity of 'the homosexual'.[19] Desire is one thing; identification with a particular social position and sense of self is quite another. Adrienne Rich, in her famous essay 'Compulsory Heterosexuality and Lesbian Existence',[20] argues that lesbian identity is not defined by sexual practice. This identity for her is partly a matter of choice.

I would like, however, in the remainder of this paper, to discuss sexual desire and not sexual identity. A weak case can be made that there is a biological, perhaps even a chemical, aspect to sexual desire which renders questionable both the existential notion of 'choice' and the view that this desire is wholly 'created' by social processes. One point is that the human species as a whole – until in vitro fertilization becomes the norm – might be said to need the expression of heterosexual 'sex drive' if it is to survive. There is, therefore, a species-specific drive which is biologically based. Of course, the point might be made that the fact that we need heterosexual contact for species survival does not imply the existence of a drive for that. The notion of a species-specific drive need not imply, however, that it is necessarily manifested in the same way in all members of the species. If there were no such thing, then there would be no biological imperative towards survival of the species, which would be contrary to Darwinian assumptions. Secondly, all human beings are born, as the 'biological' Freud emphasized, with certain instincts or drives that seek release. At least some of these are sexual in character. The drives are both partly biological and universal to the human species. The 'hydraulic' model of sexuality is both plausible to a certain degree and corroborated by the behaviour of babies and young children.

Sexual constructivists might argue against these points. Some feminists put forward the view, for example, that the *experience* of motherhood varies so much across cultures that one cannot talk of a common phenomenon; the same, it might be asserted, applies to sexual 'drives'. These are experienced in such diverse forms that one cannot speak of one phenomenon. I would, however, contest both parts of this argument. Despite the fact that the experience of motherhood varies so much for an African peasant and an American academic, there is, I believe, a shared common core: the experience of caring for a child. I would argue that there are commonalities in all such experiences – the feelings for the child, the devotion of the very young child towards its carer. This experience is inflected in many different ways, but if it is argued to be radically different in all cases, then the notion of shared experience of any kind must be abandoned, and one would not be able to talk of the phenomenon 'motherhood'. As Wittgenstein put it, long ago, a language that is wholly private is not a language at all. The same kind of point applies in the case under consideration – there is a shared core to the drives of all young children. All, as Freud argued, seek release, and all are directed upon some object or other (the breast, the bottle, the thumb, etc.). No one of them, at this stage, is obviously differentiable from any of the others.

Many sexual constructivists tend to see sexuality and sexualities as too malleable. Human bodies, for some, are in danger of slipping altogether out of the picture. On one reading of Jeffreys, as we have seen, sexuality becomes a matter of free will, of free choice. The human being, for her, is ultimately the *homo economicus* of liberal contract theory: there are no sexed bodily human beings interacting with one another, there are only free-floating wills, taking on sexual identities and sexual desires as they wish. But there is a tendency for less radical sexual constructivists to share this perspective, for they assume that human nature is plastic and mouldable. Liberal social constructivist environmentalists castigate as 'biological determinism or essentialism' any assumption that human beings have natures or bodily drives (including sex drives). 'Sexuality socialization theory' relies on a picture of human beings as blank slates or pieces of putty. Sexualities are donned under the influence of prevalent discourses – Roman Catholicism, etc. – and reinforced, like patterns of behaviour. Any differences between people – for instance, differences in gender and sexual orientation – are said to be due to culture and conditioning, and are thought to be eliminable by changing the force of present social conditioning. The argument that sexual reproduction, sexual response and sexual identity are malleable and environmentally created and that the only alternative is a kind of biological determinism is a version of the classic distinction between 'pure freedom' and 'total determinism' or that between 'reason versus passion'. There are plenty of examples of these dualisms in operation in sexual constructivists' writings: Plummer, for instance, contrasts the 'drive-based sexologic'[21] with a 'social constructivist' position, whereby sexuality is akin to a 'learned script'; another constructivist, Hastrap, in analysing the concepts of virginity and abortion, contrasts the limited role of physiological realities with multiple social and symbolic meanings.[22] Weeks posits a similar dualism in his division between 'biological essentialism' and 'social constructivism'.

One problem with these dualisms, as many feminists have pointed out, is that they have tended to be associated, in the history of western philosophy, with other dualisms – like that between 'mind' and 'body' – which privilege one side of the divide over the other. The privileged aspect mind/reason/freedom – in the thought of the ancient Greeks, for example, or in that of Francis Bacon, in a very different fashion but with many other thinkers, too – has been associated with masculinity.

To emphasize the mind/reason/freedom aspect of the duality, as do some sexual constructivists, is to reinforce this privileging of the mental over the bodily aspect of the self, and to contribute to the undermining of the domain – the 'natural' realm – which has traditionally been associated with the feminine. Until the seventeenth century, in western thought, the conception of nature as living and material was commonplace.

I would like to return, at this point, to Foucault. Some readers of Foucault might fail to recognize his work in my earlier description of him, because he has often been presented (and sometimes denigrated) as doing the opposite. Many critics of Foucault have described as unacceptable what they see as his one-dimensional account of the self as a passive, docile body, his denial of the capacity for rational and autonomous thought. Rorty sees him as taking on an irresponsible 'anarchic Nietzcheanism'.[23] Ian Wright views Foucault's thought as a 'counsel of despair' which rejects any idea of progress in history. On this reading of Foucault, he is the prime progenitor of anti-Enlightenment thinking; he sets out to counterpose the idea of the body to the Enlightenment rational, self-reflective subject and to privilege the emotions, the passions and needs over rational thought. Foucault, in his extensive investigation of bodies and their pleasures, exposes, as Nancy Fraser has put it: 'the undue privilege modern Western culture has accorded subjectivity, sublimation, ideality and the like.'[24] Foucault, throughout his writings, analyses the operations of the multifarious discourses of power – the dominant theorizations of punishment, madness and sexuality – on the body. It is this aspect of his work that has been vital for feminism. His insistence on the body as a historical and culturally specific entity has been enormously significant. One of the ways, many feminists argue, in which his thought has been significant for feminism is in its conceiving of the body as a concrete, material phenomenon without reducing this materiality to a fixed biological essence. Some notion of the body, it has been argued, is central to analysis of the oppression of women, because it is upon the biological distinction of the sexes that gender inequality has come about.

I do not want, for a moment, to underestimate the significance of Foucault's work in this regard. It has prepared the way for much feminist work that enables a re-thinking, for example, of the sex/gender distinction (where gender is seen to inform and influence one's 'sex'); and for detailed work on particular historical and cultural inflections of the female body – for example, Lucy Bland's work on the relation between women's sexuality and medical discourses in the nineteenth century. However, I would argue that Foucault's work can be read as accentuating dualism. It can be read this way because it adds the domain of the sexual – the emotions and desires – to the 'discursive' or 'mentalistic' realm. Sexualities are analysed by Foucault, both archaeologically and genealogically, primarily in terms of power relations of domination. The modern subject is constituted as object of knowledge partially through these discourses. While, in one sense, this undercuts the Cartesian dualism of reason/emotion, or mind and body, in another sense it reinforces it by contributing to the downgrading of the biological and the natural domain. The emotional is reclassified as socially constructed and rational, in this sense; it is the effect of 'discursive' forces – Christianity, classical Greek thinking – that have been socially and culturally created. In another sense, Foucault's work has been criticized for underplaying the rational dimension – the realm of the individual rational agent who is capable of responding to and resisting those dominant cultural forces. But the latter, important point, does not undermine the claim that he is also emphasizing a rational dimension of desire and emotionality which, in a sense, plays into the hands of a kind of dualism.

I would argue that pre-constructivist writing about sexuality should be re-analysed, not as many recent writers have done to demonstrate its heavily constructed character, but to point out the effect of one dimension of it as a 'natural' phenomenon. This dimension emerges from a look at Plato's *Symposium*.

Sexuality: Another View

In his *Symposium*, Plato presents a view of the nature of love.[25] He models an account of the human experience of love on homoerotic infatuation. This feature of the book has led some commentators, from Aristotle on, to dismiss it:

> Speculations of this kind belong to natural rather than moral philosophy, and may be dismissed as irrelevant to our present enquiry. Let us look at the human side of the question – all those parts of it which have a bearing on conduct and the emotions.[26]

Aristotle, perhaps, upheld a version of biological determinism about sexuality; it was quite separate from the field of emotions.

For Plato, homoerotic desire is itself an experience of 'spiritual' intercourse; indeed, the ultimate 'non-earthly' object of love – the love of beauty – is revealed through it. Plato has been blamed for a spirituality which reduces everyday objects of love to a means to an end, or allows them to be loved only as symbols of a higher reality.[27] There is something in this claim, and it is undoubtedly true that the dualism to which I objected earlier is present in Plato (it is instigated by him, after all), and yet there are insights in Plato's writing on love which provide a powerful antidote to the constructivists' picture.

Plato presents a picture of a relationship between an adolescent boy and an older man which is intense, sentimental and unconsummated. (Not all speakers in the dialogue, however, share the view of Plato's that this love should be unconsummated.)

Phaedrus, the first spokesperson, presents the idea that love is a sort of frenzy. This is a constant theme in the text: love is manic, irrational, potentially destructive. A person in love – and all loves involve desire and passion – is the opposite of the Stoic ideal of calm self-sufficiency. Love's irrationality, indeed, leads ultimately to death. Many cultural myths – Romeo and Juliet, Abelard and Heloise, Bonny and Clyde – have played upon this theme. Many writers, too, from de Sade through Freud to Bataille, emphasize the connection between eroticism and death. De Sade removes all 'others' in his pursuit of the limits of sexual desire. As Bataille puts it: de Sade 'makes his heroes uniquely self-centred, the partners are denied any rights at all; this is the key to his system.'[28]

Aristophanes, another of Plato's spokespeople in the *Symposium*, reaches Phaedrus's conclusion. He recounts how, originally, human beings were spherical objects, which were subsequently split in two, leaving each half to seek out its other. This pursuit is love, which is therefore a form of nostalgia. (Is Lacan's theme of desire as involving an unconscious seeking after a return to unification with the mother not a return to this theme?) The merging of the two sections together, however, leads to death.

For Socrates, love does not lead to death; rather it moves one on. Love as a kind of desire implies deficiency; what one loves, one desires, and what one desires, one lacks. Desire, therefore, is always unfulfilled; sentimental, unconsummated homosexual attachments provide the ideal image of the perpetual yearning he describes.

In the *Symposium*, there is an 'ascent' of loves, which parallels the 'growth' of the mind in the cave and line metaphors in the *Republic*.

> This is the right way of approaching or being initiated into the mysteries of love, to begin with examples of beauty in this world, and using them as steps to ascend continually with that absolute beauty as one's aim, from one instance of physical beauty to two to all, and from oral beauty to the beauty of knowledge, until from knowledge of various kinds, one arrives at the supreme knowledge whose sole object is that absolute beauty, and knows at last what absolute beauty is.[29]

Love, for Plato, is what life is all about, because life is a drama of escape from the gross, transient and illusory existence to a domain of truth, beauty and permanence.

Plato does not really explain how the steps up the rungs of the ladder to appreciation of absolute beauty take place. And this aspect of his theory need not detain us here. Other parts of his theory are important for present purposes.

One is his emphasis on the madness, the frenzy of sexual desire. This focus is borne out by much writing on the subject. Many writers have emphasized how, when we fall in love or when we desire another, we experience a loss of control, a sense of helplessness, an inability to make clear, rational decisions. Falling in love, as one writer put it, 'is individualistic, objectifying, linked to escapist notions of romantic love'.[30] The overwhelming feeling when 'in love' is of intense, uncontrollable emotion.

This aspect of sexual desire brings to light some limitations of one type of 'constructivism' about sexuality. Even if sexual identity can be willed, sexual desires cannot. Sexual desires cannot be willed or chosen because, by their very nature, they lay partly outside the domain of will and conscious control. This does not necessarily place them, Cartesian fashion, on the 'outside' of reason, in the domain of madness[31] (see Rosi Braidotti for readings of madness in Foucault, Lacan and Descartes as reason's 'other'), because actual desire never involves the total loss of control, the complete suppression of rational faculties. For the other side of love, as Plato puts it, is its ability to move on, to transcend the limitations of the present. Indeed, it is allowing wholly irrational desires to take a hold of a man that has produced wholly 'objectified' forms of sexual desire. But, as the recent furore over Paddy Ashdown in the UK, and Bill Clinton in the USA, has revealed once more, no sexual desire is wholly 'rational', where this means that it appears to fit in with the individual's best interests and (other) desires. Thus it cannot be wholly a matter of conscious will. Nor, however, can it be 'a product of social and historical forces'. The unconscious, irrational side to it means that it often manifests itself in ways that run contrary to these 'social and historical forces.' It is often out of tune with the person's rationally held beliefs, and with the 'discourses' including the 'bodily' discourses in which the individual is intertwined. It may, indeed, undermine these beliefs and these discourses. This sexual desire is closer to the Reichean 'involuntary pleasurable contractions' than it is to being the effect of discourses of power.

Foucault recognizes this side of sexuality; yet, at times, he appears to want to reject it as an 'inferior', rather 'dirty' form of sexuality. In the discussion with Sennett, 'Sexuality & Solitude', he quotes Augustine as saying (in *The City of God*) that in 'the sexual act', the body is shaken by terrible jerks, and one loses control of oneself. He says: 'The surprising point is not that Augustine would give such a classical description of the sexual act, but the fact that, having made such a horrible description, he then admits that sexual relations could have taken place in Paradise before the Fall.'[32] The rationalist version of control seems strongly to influence Foucault. 'Sex in erection', according to Foucault, 'is the image of men revolted against God. The arrogance of sex is the punishment and consequence of the arrogance of man.'[33] The 'problem' of sexuality becomes, for Christians (and for Foucault, too, it appears), the 'problem of the relationship between one's will and involuntary assertions'.[34] The question of sexual desire becomes part of the will itself. It is treated as a mental phenomenon. Sexuality is curiously disembodied, disconnected from the lived experiences of men and women. Foucault, then, appears to see the frenzied side of sexuality as wholly negative.

Plato uses the metaphor of the ladder for love, as he does for the mind's pursuit of knowledge. One aspect of this metaphor, I have already suggested, may be both implausible and irrelevant to the present discussion. But the idea that the lover may experience desires that lead beyond the everyday, the commonplace, is surely an important one. For Foucault, 'constructivist' sexuality is the paradigm case of individual subjection; discourses on sexuality provide one of the most powerful means to control and discipline the embodied subject. Sexuality is the vehicle of power, a power which is omnipresent. Foucault is critical of the hypothesis of the 'liberation' of sexuality, because he refutes the notion that sexuality was ever repressed. For him the law is constitutive of desire and desire lies within the system of power. In his writings, there is no space for the bodies themselves and what 'discourses' would represent for them. Foucault tends to denigrate what Grosz has called 'the lived body' – the body and its needs and desires – even as he gestures towards a bodily desire through his talk of surveillance and discipline, which implies that there is a body to be liberated.

The Platonic reading of desire allows for a different perspective. It need not lead back to a Reichean notion of 'sexual liberation' as the freeing of repressed desires. Rather, reading Plato liberally, the suggestion may be made that sexual desire may be liberating because it may unblock the hold of 'repressive' socio-cultural norms. In the social domain, in the 1960s, the 'sexual liberation movement' functioned to reveal politically repressive aspects of the family, of some aspects of state policy, etc. Those who have assumed lesbian or gay identities have helped dispel any cultural norm that relies on the 'naturalness' of heterosexuality. At a purely individual level, allowing free expression to sexual desire may function to 'free' the person from beliefs that may actually have had a constraining effect. In psychoanalysis, sexual emotions may be brought to the surface and allowed expression, and then the 'patient' may be helped to overcome difficulties in life.

There are unconscious and irrational elements to sexual love and desire which are down-played by the too 'rational' model of the 'social constructivists'. A person's sexual identity is no more created by 'discourses' – Catholicism, medicine, etc. – than rapists are 'created' by porn. Sexual desires, predilections and fantasies subvert and often contradict social realities and rationally accepted values. Many a feminist who pours scorn on the adoption of any kind of masochistic role for herself in sexual relations, or other relations with people, fantasizes her lover dominating her/beating her, in order to heighten her arousal. No desire or fantasy operates 'outside' the socially constructed individual, in this sense, therefore. But the sorts of desire I am now describing are precisely those that can contradict accepted social norms and cannot, therefore, be the creations of them. Far from being the creatures of particular Foucauldian dicourses of power, they are much more akin to the Reichean natural, or involuntary, pleasureable contractions of the Freudian drives or energy seeking release.

The 'social constructivist' picture of sexuality connects readily with a negative view of sources of erotic fantasy such as pornography. It paints a picture of sexuality as malleable, permeable, pliable, subject to manipulation by the conscious self (Jeffreys) or by social forces (Weeks and Foucault). The sexed self is viewed as akin to a social role that can be donned or removed either at will (Jeffreys) or by appropriate conditioning (Weeks and Foucault). In this sense, it is allied with certain feminist attempts to suppress outlets – like porn – for the enhancement or expression of sexual fantasies. Such feminists believe that rapists are created and moulded by pornographic imagery, and that pornography plays a major role in the legitimizing of these sorts of sexual act. I would argue, on the contrary, that the desire on the part of a man to rape a woman is much more likely to have a complex set of causes – some unconscious, some conscious. Rapists will not disappear with the eradication of pornography any more than necrophiliacs or practitioners of SM would be eliminated were we to do away with Catholicism, medicine, psychiatry, etc. Weeks and Foucault make a very important point: namely that the presence of certain social forms and 'discourses' – like psychiatry – legitimizes discrimination against particular groups of people, not only homosexuals. But this point can be made without the much stronger claim that sexual identities are created by these social forms.

Foucault has been criticized for underrating the potential of the law to protect as well as limit individuals' freedom in respect of the stance he took on rape. He argued that rape should be decriminalized and treated as an act of violence, rather than a sexual act. Yet it is easy, in a constructivist framework, effectively to deny the agency of rapists. Rapists, instead of being seen to be responsible for what they do, can be viewed as the passive 'victims' of one of the discourses of power – in this case, pornography. Andrea Dworkin's work on pornography, by blaming pornography for acts of abuse against women, has this effect. Pornography, for her, becomes a Foucauldian discourse of power. Similarly, in the work of constructivists – and Andrea Dworkin falls into this camp on this issue – women working in the sex industry lose all agency. They become 'victims' of the power–knowledge complex: pornography. Their ability to choose what they do is lost. In fact, neither rapists, on the one hand, nor sex workers, on the other, are victims; rather, both are agents actively choosing what they do.

7
The Small Matter of Children

NETTIE POLLARD

The British feminist movement has never really addressed the issue of children's liberation. In the late 1960s and early 1970s, the women's liberation movement immediately recognized that women's oppression was directly tied to the dependence of children upon them, and some feminists, especially in North America, recognized that unless children were given more autonomy themselves, the pattern of oppression would continue.

There were two issues that were of paramount concern for these women. The first was that the process of teaching girls – and indeed all children – blind acceptance of sexist doctrine began in keeping children dependent and ignorant, emotionally, physically and economically. The second was that as long as children needed constant supervision and protection, women were always most likely to be expected to fulfil this role.

In Britain and in many parts of the North American feminist movement, only the latter problem has ever generated much interest. Bringing men into the child-rearing process was one part of the answer, and day-care facilities have been a major issue on this front as well. But this approach isn't aimed at freeing children from their vulnerability to the abuse of individual and institutionalized adult power. In truth, this has been no more than a vain attempt to make women more equal with men – vain, because as long as children remain in their subordinated position, they will only grow up to replicate the sexist patterns of their elders.

With the emergence in Britain of Women Against Violence Against Women (WAVAW) in the late 1970s and, later, the feminist anti-pornography groups, some influential parts of the women's movement started to see all sex as male violence. So it should be no surprise that they would consider children victims or potential victims of male sexual violence, rather than addressing children's own desires and autonomy. The movement would sometimes even cooperate with the most vicious arms of the patriarchal state, such as the Obscene Publications Squad (OPS). In August 1990 the feminist magazine *Spare Rib*, under the headline 'Child Porno Ring Uncovered', ran a scare story of the sort more normally seen in the tabloids, urging readers to report information about the deaths of children in 'snuff' movies to the police. It favourably reported that the OPS had gathered a list of 3,000 'known paedophiles and associates'. To date, no 'snuff' movie, (i.e. where actors are actually killed), has been discovered by police anywhere in the world. No bodies have ever been discovered, and 'Operation Orchid' seems to have disappeared, but fear and loathing have been implanted in women's minds. In Great Britain, feminist work on child sexuality is rare. Tuppy Owens argues, in *The Betrayal of Youth*,[1] that children may not be harmed by the expression of their sexuality, but this is an exception.

In the United States the issue is at least sometimes part of the feminist agenda. Joan Nestle touches on intergenerational sex, as well as writing about her own experiences as a child, in her series of essays *A Restricted Country*.[2] In *Pleasure & Danger*, Gayle Rubin's 'Thinking Sex: Notes for a Radical Theory of the Politics of Sexuality',[3] tackles the issue of stigmatized sexualities, including cross-generational sex, and argues that feminists should support these types of sexualities. In the same book, Mary S. Calderone presents evidence of children's sexuality from birth, in 'Above and Beyond Politics: The Sexual Socialization of Children'. In another chapter, 'Beyond Politics? Children and Sexuality', Kate Millet looks at children's right to sexual expression in the context of their powerlessness in society, and looks forward to a time in the future when she hopes children will be able to have sex, not only with one another, but also with adults, without the fear of exploitation.

Feminist attorney and mother Eileen Scheff, addressing a North American Man/Boy Love Association press conference in 1992, argued that, 'The current witch-hunt against NAMBLA has nothing to do with protecting children. Denying youth their sexuality will not stop child molestation. Our children need social and economic power to fight back against all abuse.'[4]

In the early to mid-1970s, two groups representing school pupils emerged in Britain. They were: the National Union of School Students (NUSS), which made demands such as the abolition of school uniforms and caning, and who organized sizeable demonstrations, also attended by some teachers; and the Schools Action Union, a highly militant Maoist group which flourished for a time, especially in London. But members of both groups were almost exclusively from secondary rather than primary schools, as younger children have less access to the educational and material resources necessary for publishing, and of course they aren't allowed to come and go as they please to meetings and demonstrations. And children are not encouraged to view themselves as people with rights.

These groups dissolved by the end of the decade, primarily because leading members left school and others, for whatever reason, did not replace them. And, in the case of the NUSS, the fact that many of their demands were at least partially met reduced the impetus for their existence.

In Ann Arbor, Michigan, near the US-Canadian border, Youth Liberation (YL) was publishing a slim book (*Youth Liberation*, Times Change Press, 1972) and a quarterly magazine called *FPS*. YL directed its energies much more specifically to the position of children in society, to sexism and to the oppressive nature of the family as an institution. They published information about birth control, analysed the use of drugs to control hyperactive children, and discussed the economic dependence of young people on their parents. Again, however, as its most active members grew into legal adulthood, and some of the more obvious restrictions on school students and minors (e.g. dress codes, legal curfews on minors, etc.) were lifted, the organization disappeared.

In 1970–71 the Gay Liberation Front Youth Group was formed in Britain. It is almost inconceivable now in the age of section 28, but this group was not only unfunded, but entirely run by males and females under 21, with no lower age limit. This was a militant, angry group, demanding their liberation and committed to fighting ageism in the Gay Liberation Front.

Nevertheless, it was rare to see someone under 16 at a meeting. It's not that boys and girls do not identify as gay and want to meet others, but without 'coming out' to supportive parents, how could younger people get to meetings? How would they have the money to travel? How would they explain their absence? And, for that matter, how would they get to know of the existence of the group? (These days, lesbian and gay organizations who advertise in pop magazines and put stickers in public places get a surprising number of enquiries from under-16s.)

At the height of the movement for sexual freedom, the underground sex and politics magazine *Oz* published a complete issue written and produced by people who were under 18 years old. The three adult editors were arrested for conspiracy to corrupt public morals, and *School Kids' Oz* was declared obscene. (Their conviction for obscenity was quashed on appeal in 1972.) This case introduced an interesting concept in sexuality: that something produced by 'kids' could corrupt the morals of adults.

In the ensuing years we've gone from a complete denial that sex is an issue for children at all to thinking that children are constantly under threat of molestation, abduction and abuse. Feminists have helped us recognize that abuse is a real issue, although the understanding that it is primarily a problem within the family seems to have declined over the last decade and only recently reappeared. What is not addressed at all is the fact that children themselves are sexual and may wish to express that sexuality.

Far from being 'innocent' and becoming sexual at puberty, as was once the common belief, it is now indisputable that everyone is sexual, even before birth. Erection in males is detected in the womb from 29 weeks; erection in females, of course, is harder to detect. But baby boys are born with erections and girls with genitals swelling and vaginal lubrication. The vagina is responsive sexually from birth in cyclic lubrication. Masters and Johnson found that lubrication resulted from sexual stimulation in baby girls. Clearly, birth contains elements of sexual arousal for babies. Babies often react sexually when being held, or in other moments of physical pleasure. Reaction akin to orgasm has been detected in babies only a few months old, though masturbation and orgasm are rarely detected before the ages of one or two, and not all children masturbate.[5]

The fact that many children do masturbate and do have orgasms is undeniable, though it occurs at an age when children are not generally recognized as having sexual feelings, let alone being able to have sexual experiences. Kinsey reports that in a recent study of parents of six- and seven-year-olds, adults said that 52 per cent of their sons engaged in sex play with other boys, and 34 per cent of sons played sexually with girls; 37 per cent of daughters engaged in activities with girls, and 35 per cent with boys. These activities included looking at each other and exploring each others' bodies, attempts at intercourse, and the insertion of objects. Naturally, this survey covers only behaviour that was observed, recognized and admitted to by parents. If these figures seem amazingly high, one can only wonder at the extent of undetected sexual experience between children.

In 1991 the Family Planning Association revealed that 35 per cent of girls and 46 per cent of boys said they'd had sexual intercourse before 16, the legal age of consent in Britain. Remember, this extraordinarily high figure excludes same-sex relations and all non-coital sex. It really is no longer possible to claim that people under 16, even girls, are 'innocent' and uninterested in sexual matters.[6]

Yet the current moral panic about child abuse has pushed back our recognition of children as sexual actors rather than as merely victims. Denial of children's sexuality, and the fear that they may be sexually attacked, in fact makes them far more vulnerable to abusive situations. If children are informed about their bodies and how they function, and about what sexuality is, this awareness, in itself, means that children can be much less easily led into unwelcome situations by ignorance of what is really going on. If children know that their bodies and sexuality are their own and should be under their own control, and that sex is not forbidden or dirty, then they are much more confident when it comes to getting what they really want and refusing what they don't want. In the event of a genuine assault or abusive situation, children who are not taught that sex is shameful can much more easily come forward, report the situation and get something done about it.

If we look at the case of adult women and rape, we can see a parallel. The percentage of rape victims reporting the assault has vastly increased in this country since the 1950s, because women are now far less likely to be seen as 'sluts' or 'asking for it' when they have been sexually assaulted. In the 1950s, women who were raped were sometimes locked in mental hospitals, as were 'unmarried' mothers. Just as those women before us were afraid of the consequences of 'admitting' to any kind of sexual experience – even one that was forced – so children today prefer not to arouse adult reaction to any indication that they have been involved in forbidden activity.

Despite adult assurances to the contrary, children know that when they get 'into trouble' their word is seldom taken by adults. More than one child has been punished by a parent or other authority figure for fighting or for some other infraction when in fact they were the victim of a (non-sexual) assault by another child. Children are familiar with the experience of trying to call adult attention to their victimization, only to be punished for lying or causing the already painful events. Indeed, some girls have been blamed and thrown out of their own homes by their mothers when sexual abuse by the father has been discovered.[7]

There is a seamless pattern in the lives of children in which they are told over and over to submit to unwanted instructions and intrusions by adults – going to school, going to church, going to bed early, getting up when they don't want to, wearing clothes they don't like, eating food that's distasteful to them, etc. – and yet suddenly, when it comes to sex, we expect them to behave in a way that is completely inconsistent with everything they've been taught. This is what makes the issues of sexuality and abuse particularly difficult and confusing for children – it treats sex as a very peculiar thing indeed.

When sexual activity involving a child is discovered, whether it was assaultive or consensual, the resulting flurry of panic, anger and often hysteria from adults is frightening. If the matter is reported to the police, a train of events may be set in motion which is then impossible to stop and which may, in fact, cause severe damage to the child's life.[8] Children are often whisked off by police and social workers to strange, unpleasant buildings where unknown adults poke and pry at them for endless hours. In England, the age of criminal responsibility is ten (in Scotland it is eight), and, therefore, anyone over that age can be prosecuted for a sexual offence.

If a young partner over the age of criminal responsibility is prosecuted and the older partner pleads not guilty, the child will be subjected to intimate questioning which will be used in evidence against the defendant. If this has been a case of mutual sexual pleasure, the child has the further misery of knowing a friend will be taken away and possibly locked up because of this evidence – and children frequently blame themselves. If it is believed that the child has been in any way a willing participant in sexual activity, it is possible that she or he will be taken into care. This is the ultimate irony, since children may be in real danger of sexual assault once they are placed in children's institutions.

If the perpetrator is the child's father, mother, or other breadwinner, and is sent to prison, this may also mean that the family will have to start living on social security, or even lose their home. Children may be directly blamed by the remaining parent, and may also blame themselves, as often happens.

As far as the legal system is concerned, there is no distinction between mutual, consensual sexual relationships involving children, and actual assault. According to law, even the most eager and sexually experienced 15-year-old boy is deemed to have been incapable of consent to sex with any male or female lover over 16. Claiming consent does not protect the older person – rather, it may only make life more miserable for the younger one. In other words, it is better for the 'child' if he pretends he was abused.

This is a fairly clear demonstration that age of consent laws are no protection to children – in fact, they do quite the opposite. Child abuse happens regardless of the law; the consent law functions primarily to punish consensual acts. Our assumption that any sexuality involving a person under the age of consent must necessarily be 'abuse' leads us to act in ever more extreme and punitive ways toward those we treat as their 'victimizers' – thus, the law allows the jailing of 21-year-old males whose lovers are men perhaps only a few months short of their twenty-first birthdays, on the presumption that this is child abuse! And none of this has any helpful effect whatsoever when it comes to real assaults on children, where the abusers are left entirely undisturbed by these laws.

Young children may not express their sexuality in quite the same way as adults, but it's quite obvious that they often do wish to be sexual in some ways, and with or without society's permission, they find those ways. So what do we think we accomplish by trying to restrict this behaviour? We may make them feel guilty, we may keep them from dealing effectively with issues of birth control and prevention of disease, but we are in no way serving the needs of children.

Creating an atmosphere in which sex is understood to be acceptable in a non-violent, non-coercive, mutual environment does not teach children to accept brutal assaults; ignorance supported by scare tactics does not arm children against exploit-ative adults. Yet, in this over-protective and paternalistic time, scare tactics have become our sole means of 'protecting' children. We accept attacks on gays or on the porn industry because we have been conned into believing that somehow suppressing sexual adventure and deviance will automatically – illogically – provide some safety for children. It won't.

Yet merely eliminating harmful age of consent laws will not be sufficient to make children safe and free. To achieve this, children need social and economic power, as well as respect, in every sphere of life, for their needs and desires. Children must be taught as early as possible that their opinions matter, that their experience is valid, and that their bodies are their own possessions, so that they can defend themselves against psychological, economic and physical abuses. Just as women couldn't be autonomous while they were virtually owned by their husbands – we couldn't own our own money, and it was entirely legal for husbands to beat and rape us – so children are left dependent and victimized by the present situation. Until children have economic power and the right to make their own decisions about choices ranging from schools, clothes and food to friendships and sexuality, children, like women, will not have sexual autonomy.

8

Sex On My Mind

TUPPY OWENS

For as long as I can remember, I have been crazy about boys, and my enthusiasm has paid off, bringing me awesome times and allowing me to enter fascinating worlds. Somehow, I've always managed to get accepted as 'one of the boys', without having to ditch many of the exciting thrills of being female (dressing up, being delicate and intuitive, sexy and romantic – all those girlie things that have just become revalidated by the tranny scene that's recently emerged). It has been said of me that I am very masculine in some ways, especially sexually, but that's probably because I've related to men on many levels and picked up the best bits of their sexuality for myself. The most exciting sex, in my view, is what happens between two men. I guess I want to look like a girl and fuck like a man.

My first boyfriend invited me to join him while he was working out in the Serengeti, in East Africa. There I was, living in the middle of that vast plain with three dishy male ecologists, at the tender age of 17. I'd packed this white flowing nightie and negligee that I'd bought in Oxford Street, because I wanted something sexy to wear to lose my virginity. It all happened under a mosquito net to the muted sounds of zebra hooves and locals speculating in Swahili outside the window about whether penetration had yet occurred. I'd wear the translucent ensemble over breakfast, which would start at seven with my boyfriend, extending to when the Belgian scientist rose, and would still be going at ten when the lazy German was still downing his coffee. When all the men had started work, I'd play a few tapes (I was dead corny and brought 'The Lion Sleeps Tonight' over with my Buddy Holly and Elvis), and then slip into my dress (never been a one for overalls) to start working on the little survey I'd been delegated to do. This survey was attempting to estimate the number of each species of game on the plain by the quantity of their dung dropped per metre. See – men haven't exactly treated me like a sissy!

Then, after university, I was doing a pretty naff job in ecological research admin, but going out with this dynamic whiz kid whose dad had a printing works. I was intrigued to go and watch the big machines in action, and it was there that I first set eyes on a sex book. It was a mag – what they called in those days a 'five bob art', and I thought it was pathetic. It lacked passion, beauty, imagination. I thought it was an insult to sex. So I offered to take some pictures that would express sexuality as I pictured it. I'm sure the guys at the printers were quite amused – they already thought I was some ignorant academic who hadn't a clue about what life was about, and they were right. I was a gullible girlie in an ocean of north London porno gangsters!

Perhaps I should go back in time and tell you about *my* dad. He was hyperactive and always cracking sexy jokes. He treated me exactly the same as my four brothers, and we were all encouraged in whatever we wanted to get involved in. Unlike some daughters, I never needed to 'play up to Daddy', so I never learnt how to flirt (a big gap in my education, I've always thought). I was skinny and flat-chested at a time when Dad and the rest of the world believed Marilyn Monroe was the only real woman. I've only just started feeling my body is sexually attractive, although I've always been told that having legs going up to my chin was quite appealing. I don't think it's been much of a handicap having a humble view of my own body; in fact, I suspect that having a gorgeous body is probably better as a fantasy than a reality. I think it would be a good idea to set up alternative clinics beside all the plastic surgery clinics – Enhancement of the Self in Fantasy clinics.

As well as his full-time teaching job, Dad ran a busy wedding photography company, and we were all expected to help – taking pics, developing, and sorting photos into albums, etc. Normal British children have to help with the housework, but we also helped with the business. I hated this work ethic and was embarrassed that my dad was such a maniac (but here I am, years later, working night and day and obsessed with my passions). However, it did mean that I had money of my own from an early age, which gave me independence. I also gained early confidence – if you talk to any photographer, they will tell you that wedding photography is extremely hard work. Before I'd finished my A levels, I'd photographed over 500 weddings.

So, I was quite experienced at using a Rolleiflex when I sneaked one out of my parents' house at 5 a.m. that morning and set off towards our neighbouring village of Grantchester, where I planned to take these sexy pictures of myself to show the porno men. I thought I'd need a prop, so I took an old doll. I'd forgotten that fishermen occupy the riverbanks that early, and Grantchester Meadows, my chosen venue – famous for its poetic coverage by

William Wordsworth and Rupert Brooke – was not as private a location as I'd hoped. Never mind, I set the Rollei on its tripod with an extension cable for taking my exposures, took my clothes off hoping the fishermen wouldn't notice, stuffed the dolly up my tush and swooned, eyelids heavy towards the lens.

Of course, the men laughed like a drain when they scanned my developed roll of film, and kindly informed me that pictures like this were against the law. I was very disappointed – but intrigued. I decided to leave my government post and work with them, just for a bit.

I got quite involved with producing and importing porno. I drove car loads of quasi-legal porn up to Sheffield once a week (always terrified of an M1 accident and sitting there moribund in the middle of a sea of dancing sex books), and sometimes produced magazines. I put together an issue of *Cinema X* which sold out in two days, simply because it had a photo on the cover that I'd taken of my girlfriend screwing some fella in a field. I gained a bit of respect from the hoods for that.

This was in the late 1960s when there was a sexual revolution supposedly going on around me, but I have to confess that I didn't feel as if I was part of anything revolutionary, because we were just having a great time. Being a 50s girl, I didn't relate to all that hippie shit. This was a shame, in a way, because I missed getting involved with the Wet Dream Festivals in Amsterdam, and the wild and thought-provoking magazine *Suck*, which was at that time being produced by sexual experimentalists, including Germaine Greer. I enjoyed the people I was working with – unpretentious and fearless of the law. In those days the porno squad was pretty corrupt, and I never really thought they would send you to prison for anything as trivial as producing sexy pictures. I kept my stash of favourite porn mags – including *Suck* – at the top of the lift shaft in my block of flats, just in case I got raided, and it was a sad day when the lift broke down and my stash got nicked. I liked porn then, just as I like it now, and I accepted the seedy aspect of it – sometimes wondering if being seedy helped sales, as people liked the idea of a mag being produced in a back room, smuggled, sneaked and rushed. It matched their idea of sex. I sort of liked it too, but didn't feel I could produce that kind of stuff, myself. I had this ambition to produce porno as beautiful as the pages of *Vogue*. I was dead envious when I saw Madonna's book, *Sex* – it's like what I wanted to do, all those years ago.

Sex position books were just hitting the market, but their illustrations were barely beyond sombre matchstick poses, which I knew I could improve on. So I walked up to Selfridges and bought some pretty sheets, lugged my bed into a studio, got the most popular model I could find (after asking all my mates who they liked best), and, fortunately, she had a handsome boyfriend. We had a real laugh taking the pics. I remember, when I said we'd be doing some 69 shots, the boyfriend whispered to the girl, she whispered back, and I could tell he'd never done it before, and had no idea what she meant. She must have been hoping, though, and this was her moment!

I got help writing the text because I knew I wasn't quite the average girl, sexually, and I wanted to make sure I'd be presenting a reasonable account of what sex should be like. I designed the book like a landscape magazine and called it *Sexual Harmony*. It got printed at the place in Highbury where I was working. This was at exactly the time that the Ann Summers shops were opening and in need of merchandise to appeal to women. They loved my book and it became their best seller. Only one snag: I'd done it as a laugh, and there was no money in it for me.

Never mind, I'd learnt how to do it, now knew all the people in the porno world, and decided I could make it on my own. So I left the print works, with the agreement that I'd carry on distributing my book. With the cash I earned from that, I paid some more models, took more pics, and launched my range of photo books called *Love in the Open Air*. I was never much good at studio lighting, so I took more sex position shots in selected fields, woods, playgrounds, riverbanks and traffic islands around Britain. This was strictly low-budget – the models only got paid ten pounds a day, but they did usually say it was one of the best days they'd ever had in their lives. I agreed – we went to the most fabulously beautiful places and took some lovely erotic photos. The models were a mixed bunch but always unpretentious, fun-loving, and even treated their profession with the same idealism I did. They were mostly ex-hippies who loved sex, loved posing, and told me that coming out with me was much more fun than modelling for the London Underground Photographic Club, or one of the seedy photographers who didn't care about quality and would leave the film boxes by the bed they'd be posing on.

I put prose with the photos, and Robin Ray, my partner, did the design. The books were far too gentle to compete with the male-produced porno – they sold to couples and to men who like that kind of thing. I think most people found them embarrassing, as they were very personal. They were also a bit crummy. I was getting disappointed with the way printers reproduced my photos.

It was as if sex didn't matter, so it didn't matter what my books looked like. As the print quality seemed to get worse and worse, I was also becoming disenchanted by the quality of my photography. Looking back, I must say that what my photos lacked in professional expertise, they made up for (sort of) in the entertainment value and tenderness. I still find them quite sexy. Some were used by Penny Slinger for her drawings in the big book *Sexual Secrets*, and some of those drawings, in turn, pop up in small publications and leaflets promoting various aspects of sex. So they live on, as things do.

I admit that I spent more time worrying about what the females in the pics looked like. This was partly because I thought that the female body was the more sexy, and men who were buying the books rarely seemed to care what the men looked like. I don't think I ever found a male model who looked exciting in the pics – it was as much as I could do to make them look acceptable (i.e. not repulsive), but I was sad that the men didn't look better. I assumed a man didn't come across as sexy-looking unless you already fancied him in real life or as a film star. I put this down to the fact that much of the attractiveness of a man is his personality, voice and intelligence. I don't think the same way now, but it's still not a straightforward matter of physical appearances in a photo being a turn-on, on their own; there are other influences. I think it's exciting that it's so difficult to put your finger on what it *is* about men that turns us women on.

Robin was not like the porno merchants, but a real enthusiast. He encouraged me to write the way it came out, and to take pride in what I was doing. He also introduced me to the first hard-core porno that I ever saw. He showed me a copy of *Private* and my eyes popped out of my head. I loved it and felt a bit feeble staying in soft core. But getting into hard core would mean working abroad, and, anyway, I didn't think I could cope with the hard-core photography myself; I thought work and an erection in one room would be unmanageable.

Robin was keen to go to orgies. While I'd worked with the big porno guys I'd met a man who threw sex parties, but they'd treated him with suspicion. It's strange how porno people can be quite straight. I've found that lots of people in the sex world are really limited – people into one extreme find people in other scenes unacceptable, like some swingers think the fetishists are weird and vice versa. Maybe one of the reasons I've succeeded is because I was almost the only person in the industry to stay open to everything.

Anyway, when Robin enthused for the millionth time, I agreed to take him to a sex party. It did seem to me to be an OK idea to be able to have lots of sex with loads of different people at the same time, so I got us both invited. We were both very nervous, and I would probably have fled if I hadn't found myself distinctly popular. After all, I was still only about 27, and you didn't get many single 27-year-old girls who were curious enough about orgies actually to pitch up and go for it – still don't. I got to the stage where I imagined that eventually I'd end up with this big house, hosting wonderful sex parties, but perhaps living in a gate house with my husband and two kids. This little fantasy lasted a year or two, but thank goodness I got over that one!

I did carry on going to the parties for several years, but they never lived up to what I'd hoped. The sex was perfunctory and unaffectionate, the men were good fun but utterly uncaring. I remember saying to one that I wasn't on the pill so he mustn't come inside me, and after he'd pumped his load right up me, everyone watching sang out, 'It's fine, he's an abortionist, you'll be OK.' See what I mean? Not exactly what a girl needs.

Only twice can I remember really enjoying myself – once when I found myself in the middle of eleven bisexual men with everything being penetrated everywhere (heaven! – but sadly, it would be a dire health risk these days), and the other time when I got into some heavy screwing with a guy I rather liked and respected. During our intense session I vaguely noticed that the rest of the room was going quiet. After the sex was over, I looked up, and the bed had become a stage, with everyone sitting on the floor in rows, clapping. I suppose I felt proud that without even knowing I'd given them a show they'd enjoyed. It was this kind of giving that inspired me to carry on in the sex world. I loved the fact that you could have fun and then make money out of it. I loved the idea of other people having a great time as a result of it.

I got into all kinds of projects: records, cosmetics, films large and small; I did magazine columns, produced contact mags, imported and exported. Most things flopped before they ever materialized, but I kept financially afloat. I got raided a few times and financially knocked many times. I managed to keep a pretty low profile (I'd hate to be famous). Except during very busy times, I kept myself a one-girl band. It's taxing and sometimes quite lonely, but gives you more freedom than employing people.

Lasse Braun, one of the top porno film makers of all time, invited me to take part in a half-million dollar production he was planning to shoot in Holland. It was called *Sensations* and it was the first sex film to be shot on 35 mm. I was 34 and thought my opportunity to become a porn star was now or never, as I was getting on in years. I was excited about my little role, and assumed I'd be a blast, so it was quite humiliating to find out, when the time came, that I couldn't really do it. I was a hopeless actress, hated having the camera on me, didn't like being told how to perform, detested not being able to move freely or I'd be out of focus. Well, you don't know until you try.

Sensations has become a bit of a cult movie, despite my failure – luckily, I only had a small part. But – would you believe it? – I was persuaded to be in another film, *Lady Victoria's Training*, shot in Oxfordshire. I insisted that I should have total control over what I did; that way, I thought I might enjoy it. I wouldn't let them know what that would be until I turned up. The director, Mike Freeman, was into *cinema vérité*, so that was cool, and everything would have been fine if his camera had been in working order when I arrived on set. Never mind, the 'dress rehearsals' were utterly outrageous, and the crummy final result of my performance convinced me never to darken a porno screen again.

The Sex Maniac's Diary was selling well each year, and each edition became more of a world guide to things sexual, including clubs and events, so I cornered myself a niche as international expert. Although this has its advantages, it's also a nuisance because people treat me like an automatic information bank. I've tried to present an accurate picture of the various sex scenes, to help people enter them and understand how to behave. Clubs are listed solemnly just like they would be in any other diary, which is my statement that sex is to be revered and appreciated just like any other human activity. I tend to promote quality and avoid listing rip-off joints. I've always wanted to produce Sex Maniac's Recommendation stickers for the windows and doorways of good clubs. I promote safer sex throughout. I have tried not to be censorious, and when distributors have insisted that I take out certain clubs (usually because they were self-help groups for people who are into illegal acts), I've usually carried on listing them under another name, perhaps in code. People in sexual minority groups have really appreciated my determination. I have, for example, got a lovely picture of a man kissing his new 'wife', a mare, with greetings on the back. He said that my letter to him was the only one he'd ever received that ended with the words 'Love to you and your mare.'

Back in 1979, I was approached by a friend, a psychologist, who had a patient with a sex problem. His problem was simple: he was in a wheelchair and had never had sex. He was exactly my age, and when I thought back to all the sex I'd had, I thought this was pretty appalling. I introduced him to people and discussed ways in which he might make approaches from his chair. After six months he got laid – a big day!

I already had a friend – a business client – who had lost his sight and lost all his friends as a result, and it occurred to me that people with disabilities didn't *have* to be friendless and loveless. I thought they just needed some adult link with the rest of society, to re-establish their belief in themselves by having someone who valued them as people, who might also help by acting as a model for others to follow – to accept them as physically and mentally desirable. It seemed that this very simple thing could make all the difference to that person, so they would no longer have a vile time. I decided it was something I'd like to involve myself in.

It was obvious that if the chap in the wheelchair who'd just got laid had nothing better to do, he would be the best person to run such a service. He said he would but, sadly, he didn't, and I ended up running it myself. It seemed quite a daunting thing to do, but so far there have been few tears and lots of love has grown out of it. It's called Outsiders. Outsiders is a self-help group helping people with social and physical problems to find partners and gain confidence to form relationships. My friend Vieta helped me set it all up from my basement flat in Mayfair. We offered postal and phone contacts between members, social events in restaurants and plenty of support. Vieta was determined about one thing: we wouldn't spoon-feed members. It was up to them if they made use of Outsiders or not.

Running Outsiders has been, I think, more thrilling than any of my other work. I've formed deep friendships with people I would never have known otherwise, and we've had enormous fun. There's never been that 'helped and helpers' thing in the club – just lots of people who feel outside society – and that includes me. That's not just because I don't share many of the current values (e.g. looks and money), but also because I'm shy, have suffered panic attacks, and anyway, I'm usually shunned by polite society because I'm so openly horny!

Outsiders hasn't been accepted by the established disability organizations or the radical groups of people with disabilities that have formed with the aim of running things for themselves. Separatist feminists attacked us early on in *Spare Rib*, accusing me of encouraging disabled men to behave as badly as their 'able-bodied' brothers. The *People* did a meaningless – but very effective – 'expose', and we're still slagged off just about everywhere. The public just can't accept us. It's a real shame, because it's one of the most cost-effective means of relieving suffering and bringing people pleasure that's ever been.

When my residents' association insisted I no longer run it from my flat, we got an office, which we have to pay for, but otherwise the club virtually runs itself – by members helping each other, gaining confidence, and making new friends and eventually finding partners. Outsiders welcomes anyone who completes our application form. We have as many members who have no physical disability but who are crippled by shyness, phobia or fear of the opposite sex as we do members who are blind, deaf, paralysed or disfigured, etc. The people with physical disabilities tend to help the shy with socializing, and the shy people gain confidence through helping the people who have physical problems in practical ways, like taking them to the toilet. There is no pressure to be sociable, but people become so when they are ready. I love to see people coming out of their shells – and then, when you see them in each other's arms, or hear that they're having a ball and no longer need Outsiders, it's magic.

Outsiders has worked best when we've been working together towards some aim. We put on an art exhibition called *Emotions in Focus* and have organized various campaigns to raise public awareness about the personal needs of people with disabilities. Over the years we've toned down this side, because everything we did tended to make our reputation worse, and we'd be further away from gaining support from those who might offer financial security and those who refer potential members to us. However, I miss the old days terribly. For example, one little outing springs to mind. Just before Christmas one year, we decided to go caroling to raise some funds after one of our Saturday lunches. This higgledy-piggledy trail of people (the shy pushing the wheelchairs and leading blind people, etc.) ventured round the corner into Argyle Square, near King's Cross, and accosted the johns in the street, saying they couldn't get off with the professional street whores until they'd listened to at least one carol and paid us some money. The whores were into it a lot and joined in the singing. We raised several hundred pounds in just over an hour. Well, this innocent little jaunt was probably my idea, but you can imagine how rumours might have spread afterwards, getting more and more twisted and weird as they went round the rehab wards and charity offices. I've always lived by the principle that in this hyp-ocritical society, freedom comes from blowing your reputation (so you have nothing to lose), but with Outsiders, it affects people, so I have to toe the line.

In order for Outsiders to become independent of me, it has now formed its own management committee. It also has a membership secretary to do the everyday work. Her salary is paid for by funds raised from The Sex Maniac's Ball.

The Ball is an annual event organized by me and some other sexual idealists. It's in a category of its own. I sometimes think its concept was inspired by Fellini's *Juliette of the Spirits*, which I religiously went to see every year after it came out, in the early 1960s. My original idea was to let all the sex clubs listed in the *Diary* celebrate with each other once a year, so everyone could meet. The Ball serves another very important purpose: it encourages people, whatever their sexual taste, to come and express their sexuality, knowing they will be accepted. We have, for example, a playpen for adult babies, and a tea room for people who like messy cake fights. Quite a few people with physical dis-abilities buy tickets, or get invited to accept various Outsiders awards, so the event is one big celebration of sexual integration. Over 1,000 people attend, about 150 of whom are volunteers running the fundraising side-shows.

I've never bothered with too much political stuff. I suppose I'm a good example of English empiricism, and I'm definitely not a Camille Paglia (although I agree with her on many things). I've just done my thing and avoided confrontation. To begin with, it never occurred to me that enjoyment and bringing other people pleasure would do anything other than inspire others to please and be pleased, and I was flabbergasted when I heard feminists accusing porno people of exploitation and abuse, of people thinking that desire, the spirit of sex, was wrong. I have been more and more shocked at how these attitudes have been blocking pleasure. So last year I produced a new book, *The Politically Correct Guide to Getting Laid*.

Lately, I *have* become political. This is probably because groups like Feminists Against Censorship and The SM Rights Group (which began as Countdown on Spanner) have been formed to campaign for things I believe in. Before that, we stood for sexual rights, but couldn't really do much on our own. The *Diary* has also become more political as, I suppose, I've become impatient that, after 20 years of its existence, the public are just as ignorant, if not more ignorant, about sex – and with AIDS, that's pretty dangerous.

The anti-sex moral majority groups have become bigger and more organized. Last year I was so worried I had to warn my readership: stand up to be counted, or else expect to be censored into virtual celibacy.

I don't know if this chapter has really explained things in any way to help you understand what I do and inspire you to have more fun. You've got to take responsibility for yourself, and that means having some tricks of the trade that work for you and aren't short-term hypocritical bits of shit that land you in it the next day. Here are some of the values I think have probably seen me through, so far:

- Everything ends in tears, so you may as well do it.
- Never have sex with anyone unless you're turned on/fancy them. If you have sex for money or other reasons, switch into another mode so that your desire channels remain untainted.
- Never let anyone push you into doing anything sexual that feels uncomfortable to you. If they try, push them into something else that *you* like. If you don't have the physical strength, cry, yell, explain you're unhappy.
- If you end up having a bad time, tell lots of people about how terrible it was – create your own black comedy.
- If things are imperfect with a lover (which they normally are), there are many better ways of reacting than moaning. You can make the most of them, and look around for something more suitable, or else you can discuss the way you feel in the hope that things will improve. Usually things get better or worse on their own so you don't have to make any rash decisions. One little tip: don't expect instant results when you tell your lovers something – people don't like being told what to do, or have their ignorance exposed. Just say what you want to say and then leave it. Wait a few days or weeks and then, with any luck, you'll be delighted to discover that it's sunk in and is having its effect. Or maybe they shouldn't change, anyway.
- Treasure that thing called desire. It's probably the most extreme sexual feeling you'll ever have and, whatever happens in life, they can never take your desire away. Not that it's something you can flaunt, because people easily feel pressure and embarrassment from it when you express it – just enjoy it for yourself, your own pleasure. When you find it *is* safe to express it – *wow*!

Well, that's what works for me, and it may or may not work for you. I know that some women are afraid, and it's probably no use telling you there's nothing to be afraid of. Sex is like everything else; it has its good and bad sides, it just has more good things going for it than most other things in life. I tend to try not to dwell on disasters, just laugh instead of moan, because moaning is a dreary thing to do. Generally, I either have a blissfully good time or a hilariously bad time.

Sometimes sex has made me very sad, and the saddest thing of all is the fact that I've never quite managed to be able to get *enough*. I was comforted by Sir John Betjeman, who, when asked in an interview if he had any regrets about his life, said, 'Yes, I haven't had enough sex.' I thought, well, now I can confess that, too.

But never mind – when I'm not doing it, at least I can be writing about it. The good news is, it gets better. I used to dread getting older because I thought my sex life would go down the drain, but it's still soaring. These days, sex brings me into other forms of consciousness, injects me with massive doses of what feels like rejuvenation fluid, which magically makes me feel as if I'm about eight-years-old. This is a great fuel to my fantasies and, anyway, I'm always left with a fresh complexion. Sex strengthens my bow to give energy to projects and makes me feel wonderful. I don't demand to be pleasured and pampered – I'm very aggressive and find it difficult to lie still, keep quiet or allow sex to come to an end. I like to get into long, lingering tonguing, which could be interpreted as being submissive, but my experience is that it's incredibly creative, opening highly charged channels of physical communication. Being penetrated is not, to me, a passive act, as my cunt pulls the cock inside, and that action stimulates the rest of my pussy, so that it becomes sexually charged.

I really value being single. Sex and love have never meant security or permanence to me – I equate commitment with prison. That doesn't mean lack of devotion and caring – even the maternal instinct can be very sexual. I mould my affairs to be beautiful journeys – not just soppy dinners and fucks but giving each other courage to meet new challenges. That includes enjoying new sexual experiences and going off in different directions.

Women don't need to live dreary lives – we have our own strength, we have each other and we have men. The big mistake women often make is to rely on others, usually men, rather than on our own strength. People talk about centuries of male oppression, but I look upon it as centuries of women being feeble. Also, it's stupid to think we have to be the same as men to be free. You can be tough and use your own strength and still be a housewife who's supportive and unambitious in worldly things.

I don't think that being a homemaker is anything to be ashamed of. It's hard to know how I'd *really* feel about being in that position myself, after 20 or so years of running my own thing (usually working about 18 hours a day), having all the independence (and stress) that's brought, but I crave a bit of housework, cooking, darning and lack of outside responsibility. I say, 'Send the men out to work and let's stay home with our feet up, but better still, let's all stay home!' I know I'd never have stuck with all this career nonsense if I hadn't stumbled into such compelling work (or if I'd found someone to keep me, but I'm right off rich men). I have to confess that it's easy to hold these views until I find myself in suburbia surrounded by housewives – then I have a rapid change of heart.

You may be curious to know what I think of porn, after all this time. Well, I still like it, but I'm disappointed that it hasn't moved very far. I really don't bother to look at it much. I think that porno is really only of interest when it deals with impossible things. It's rather like fantasy – no point in fantasizing about something if you can actually do it. So I guess I'm only really interested in illegal porn – the kinky stuff. I don't believe in exploitation, but fiction, illustration and computer graphics can produce images that don't involve using live models. Porno has a long way to go, which is very exciting. I hope that I will be involved when it goes there, and that the censorship in Britain won't prevent me doing so.

It's been very interesting working on these new sex mags for women. I don't think that they've got the formula right and I hope that the magazine I'm about to edit will smash barriers, turn everything on its head and open up a new world. I should confess that writing for women feels different from writing in men's magazines. For example, there was one stage when I was doing a letters column for both a men's and a women's mag, and there was one letter from a woman that I'd put in my men's mag column, and I asked the woman if it would be OK if I included it in the women's magazine, too. Then I looked at my reply and it was erotic. Putting an erotic reply to a problem letter seemed totally unacceptable in a woman's mag, as we expect replies to be earnestly helpful. This seems to be a big difference that still exists between men and women – women are into consolation, men into titillation. If you're having a bad time, women friends are supportive, men lift you up and transport you elsewhere. Anyway, back to the letter: I bunged the identical letter and reply into the women's sex mag, refusing to allow myself to treat women differently from men, but predictably, the editor never used it.

I have probably given the impression that I don't relate to women at all, but in fact I am finding some of them quite groovy these days. I enjoy working beside Di, the Outsiders' membership secretary, who's a delightful, sex-positive feminist. Many of the women I relate to, however, are not in the UK. I stay in touch with, and am loosely linked with, fellow pioneers such as Annie Sprinkle – she says I'm the British equivalent of her, which is a total exaggeration, but very complimentary. Frank Moore calls us all the Cherotic Movement – 'strong, lusty women redefining and expanding sexual, spiritual and social concepts of life, and influencing anarchic teenagers who are searching for positive values.'

One of the women I feel closest to is a friend who shares my view that men who have disabilities make the best lovers, probably because they are forced to plan, use initiative and imagination to make it possible, and thus don't just plough into it thoughtlessly. She's currently wondering if she shouldn't be lesbian, which is making me more aware of my channels of love for women. On the whole, though, I've found women haven't made the best friends for me. Even the most fiercely radical feminist friend I had wasn't seen for dust when she found a boyfriend last year. Perhaps she was just using the 'radical feminist' attitude to cover up her own insecurities, and I suspect this is often the case. There's not much point in claiming feminist values and still treating each other like second-class citizens, but I can't see how this will ever change in my lifetime. Women just don't seem to be self-propelled. I've never tried fucking a woman; I think I'd be disappointed that they didn't have a nice, juicy propeller. Yes, I'm sure I would. Sex without a dick would be pretty much a waste of time for me.

Let's hope that my sex mag, which *can't* show dicks (Smiths and Menzies won't allow them to be shown in their exciting, excited state), won't also be a waste of time. It's a travesty! Dicks are delectable, incredible biological structures. The whole apparatus, the size, the way it fits inside, and the precariousness of it all, makes me wonder why people bother to take an interest in anything else in life at all. That so many cocks go unloved and uncherished by women these days is an unbelievable waste of resources, and also senseless human cruelty.

9

Snuff: Believing the Worst

AVEDON CAROL

Perhaps the most compelling excuse for the new 'feminist' definition of 'pornography' that has gained currency in the anti-porn movement is the claimed existence of movies made by raping and murdering women in order to make films. In fact, the rhetoric that conflates this category of documentary violence with pornography – the latter being what most people understand to be sexually explicit, rather than violent, material – has been so pervasive that it is virtually impossible to have a reasoned discussion of actual pornography without firmly insisting that the 'feminist' definition be dismissed.[1] Once the word 'pornography' is used, too many listeners assume that the topic is material which is explicitly violent, degrading, and usually made by committing real acts of violence against the women who appear in the movies or photographs. Since most pornography has nothing to do with this false definition, honest attempts to discuss the dangers inherent in censoring pornography can easily collapse in confusion and acrimony as knowledgeable speakers try to discuss actual sexual material while those who have accepted anti-porn rhetoric scream in outrage at the perception that the speaker is defending the rape and murder of women just to make masturbatory materials for men. A considerable part of this attitude towards pornography, however, is based entirely on myth.

Feminist hyperbole about the violence of pornography, along with an insistence from some that there is no difference between consensual sex and rape, reached such a peak by the mid-1970s that it had nearly become impossible, in discussion, to distinguish real violence from ordinary sex. Speeches by some feminist anti-pornography speakers gave the impression that the content of even pin-up magazines was nothing more than a catalogue of butchery. A minor stir was at one point caused when, in answer to these continuous accusations, one well-known US men's magazine, *Hustler*, reacted by illustrating this charge on its cover with a picture of a smiling model being fed through a meat-grinder – rather like a statement that: 'This is what they say we do.' But anti-porn feminists did not recognize this as an attempt, however tasteless, to participate in the discourse *about* sexual material; rather, they added the cover photograph to their anti-porn slide-show presentations as a typical example of what porn depicts and what its 'real' message is. The language linking porn to genuine violence escalated to the extent that each metaphor, taken as fact, led to a belief in even greater violence in pornography, which led to even more extreme metaphors and eventually culminated in the claim that 'porn' films were circulating in which women were actually murdered in order to make the movies – 'snuff' films. The moral right, too, enjoyed capitalizing on the rumour.

The story, it seems, is that the movie *Snuff* came out in response to the rumours, and then the movie was used to confirm the rumours. We do know that, in early 1976, *Snuff* was previewed in the United States, and many people walked out of the movie house honestly believing they had seen a real killing captured on film. This was the long-awaited proof that the gory deaths of women are what men *really* fantasize about when they look at pornography and even when they have sex.

Snuff was certainly a sexploitation film of a particular B-movie subgenre which is somewhat different from pornography. In the beginning, it started off as another film, released earlier, which had failed to generate much interest. But the film makers later tacked on the famous ending in which a woman appears to be spontaneously murdered by a co-worker on the film set, while the cameras are still running.[2]

In *Hard Core*, Linda Williams offers this description:

> After the pregnant actress is stabbed, the camera pulls back to reveal a movie set with camera, crew, and director. A 'script girl' admires the director's work and tells him she was turned on by the scene. He invites her to have sex; she complies until she realizes that this scene, too, is being filmed. When she tries to pull away, the director grabs the knife from the previous scene, looks directly at the camera and says, presumably to the operator, 'You want to get a good scene?' and proceeds to slice off first her fingers, then her hand, and then the rest of her. The sequence culminates in the director cutting open the woman's abdomen, pulling out her inner organs, and holding them over his head in triumph while the sound track mixes heavy panting with the beat of a throbbing heart. The organs seem to convulse. The image goes black as a voice says, 'Shit, we ran

out of film.' Another says, 'Did you get it all?' 'Yeah, we got it. Let's get out of here.' No credits roll.[3]

The uproar over the alleged murder of women on camera in sexually explicit media ultimately led New York City's district attorney to demand that the 'victim' in *Snuff* be brought forward. In due course, she made public appearances and was interviewed in the media, but the truth never caught up with the rumours. Police departments all over the world have tried and failed to find evidence of even one 'snuff' film, but most have finally admitted that the rumours have no basis in fact.

Defenders of the 'snuff' myth point out that the failure of the police to locate something is no proof that it does not exist, but even the people who make and sell pornography, as well as porn's consumers, are baffled by the persistence of the legend of 'snuff' when none of them has even heard of a film that actually fits the bill. Campaign Against Pornography (CAP) claims 'snuff' is a widespread phenomenon; but where is it made, and who is it sold to, and how does it advertise? Surely *someone* would have heard of it by now if it really existed.

Another question arises here: given the capabilities of actors and special effects artists, why on earth would someone take the risks of committing a real murder on camera to make a film that artifice can produce even more efficiently? And since we've all grown up seeing violence portrayed on television and in film, how could a viewer 'know' they were seeing real violence when we know it can be easily faked?

A number of anti-porn writers claim they have seen a real snuff film – yet when we read their descriptions, we recognize the ending of the movie *Snuff* itself. CAP's most recent leaflet refers to 'disemboweling women' as if it were an entire genre within pornography, but again, this is merely another reference to the final scene in *Snuff*. Indeed, even if this proved not to be the case, how would a viewer *know* she had seen a real murder? Special effects are so convincing these days that the only way we can know for sure whether a death has occurred is if we see the body – something no anti-porn campaigner has claimed to have done.

Yet many people persist in believing that snuff is the ultimate in male sexual fantasy, that there *must* be millions of men out there keen to see real snuff movies and, therefore, there are producers out there who are providing them. Since there is no material evidence of such desire in men or of such films, what is the basis for that continued belief?

It should go without saying that there is something obviously out of whack in the relationships between men and women in our society, but the belief in snuff carries this to extremes. We know that some people do commit acts of hideous brutality against others, and that many of these acts occur in the context of sexual violence – but to extrapolate from this that large numbers of men necessarily wish for similarly gruesome scenarios in their ordinary sexual excursions is to embrace the most hysterically paranoid view of men and sexuality.

As others have observed, most pornography is just about men and women enjoying sex together. From this it would be reasonable to assume that what most men want sexually is to have sex with someone who would enjoy having sex with them. (And what is so terrible about that?) And much as some of our media may enjoy playing up the picture of thousands of men prowling the streets waiting to victimize violently any passing female, the truth is that most women do not spend most of our time being raped, nor even most of our time within relationships being assaulted.

We may not be able to control the emergence of rapists, wife beaters and child abusers in our society, but we might control our tongues before we suggest that the people who commit these terrible acts are *normal*. It is by no means normal for men to interpret mere sexual urges as an instruction to rape – most men don't. Nor is it normal for men to equate sexual feeling with acts of brutality. But we as a society seem to go out of our way to try to make the equation of sex with violence, to press men to feel almost as if there is something wrong with them if they don't react to sexual arousal with an urgent need to do harm. Anti-pornography campaigners lend themselves to this propaganda campaign when they insist that looking at pictures of people having sex must make men leap to thoughts of violence; there is no logical connection between erotic interaction and brutality, so where is this coming from?

Yes, there is much in our culture that encourages men to feel they should fear women and keep us down – but there is no evidence that those messages come from pornography. For thousands of years, every authority from palace to pulpit has seemed to want to reinforce the idea of female subjection and male sexual violence, and it's really no use pretending that pictures of nude humans created those ideas.

More importantly, there is also no evidence that those messages uniformly influence men. Regardless of what we may hear many men say, in practice they very seldom look like the ravaging monsters portrayed in the image of the violent, sexually uncontrollable male. Yes, some men have stupid ideas and do monstrous things, but many more men recognize that stupidity and monstrousness serve no purpose in their lives. Quite a few men are, of course, confused by the public insistence that they should somehow resemble these images when they know they don't – doesn't it do more harm than good to tell men that they are *supposed* to be rapacious villains?

As all too many women know, it is very easy, in the trauma after being abused in a relationship or even raped by a stranger, to get caught up in latching on to these gross generalizations about the evils of men. It's a nice neat explanation for the terrible things that have happened to us, and it gives us someone else to hate, someone else to blame, when we need a target for our anger. If we can project human evil onto a group we don't belong to, we can claim a kind of virtue and nobility. But this is a dangerous game that can lead to a failure to recognize our own weaknesses – some women, too, emotionally and physically abuse others, and it does no good to adhere to an ideology that says we can't really be doing the terrible things men are doing because, by definition, they are male behaviour. And we should start by recognizing that they *aren't* male behaviour; rather, they are ugly, somewhat unusual things that some human beings do to others. The extremes represented by 'snuff' do not generally occur between us, and we do everyone a disservice when we try to normalize them by claiming that they are common to all men.

It's understandable that many women are frightened, hurt and angry enough at some of the things men do that we are willing to believe the worst of men. Or maybe we suspect men of being so angry at us that they are bound to have 'snuff' fantasies. But at some point we all have to admit that reality is a lot more mundane, and that violence is not synonymous with sexual fantasy – even for men.

Yes, the idea of snuff films is a very scary one; but perhaps more scary is the fact that, even when the evidence is that no snuff film exists, we are still so willing to believe in it.

10

Fear of Pornography

CLAUDIA

> Man could not live without deceiving himself.
>
> Turgenev: *Home of the Gentry*

Fantasy makes human relations possible. It inspires people to court each other, copulate and procreate. Without romantic or sexual dreams they would find it hard to sustain the effort. If fantasies were taken less seriously, birth and marriage rates would plummet. Individuals strive to escape their own boredom and self-doubt by fixating upon other beings as the embodiment of their desires. Most make fantasy figures out of people superficially dissimilar to themselves. It is easier to ascribe imaginary qualities to an unknown entity, and harder to recognize signs that show they are as fallible as we know ourselves to be. For this reason, hetero-sexuality predominates, and my friend in Moscow believes that the man who is not tied to his mother's apron strings can be found in the west. I, too, am fairly well practised in the art of self-deception. I used to dream of someone who could share my enthusiasms yet remain free from middle-class pretension. Therefore, I planned to hang around building sites dropping copies of *Brothers Karamazov* in the hope of eliciting an enthusiastic response from a passing labourer.

'Love' and 'passion' are the products of myriad imaginings. Dreams are believed to have 'come true' when they receive social recognition and approval. The feminist likes her man to make public appearances with the baby strapped to his chest for the same reasons that the ageing rock star struts around with a young model. The 'stable relationship' receives the greatest seal of approval. Individuals are encouraged to find a being around whom they can bind every aspect of their lives. Violence, murder, mental illness and terminal boredom are the common products of such arrangements. The more unstable and dangerous the relationship becomes, the more its image is idealized. On a personal level, people believe it is their choice of partner that is at fault, rather than the absurdity of their expectations. On a wider scale, an army of professionals – many of them feminist – is employed to prop up the ideals of love and family life.

'Fighting to save one's marriage' has long been deemed a task appropriate only to the female sex. In this tradition, the majority of contemporary feminists concentrate on promoting the idyll of couplehood. They contend that eternal bliss will be attained when women become 'equal' partners, or when both partners become women. Such feminists are so threatened by anyone who does not seem to share their aspirations that they have thrown in their weight with political conservatives and religious nutcases in trying to eliminate dissent.

There is a growing tendency to portray individual fantasy as a social danger. Gay men are jailed *because* they consent to sado-masochistic practices, pornography is banned, and sex workers harassed. Like millions of other people, prostitutes earn their living through the sale of fantasies. I know a hooker of 60 who can get men to part with money by posing as a '19-year-old schoolgirl', yet she faces imprisonment next time she gets busted for advertising her services on phone-box stickers.

This woman, and all those who, like her, actively choose to work in the sex industry, are irksome thorns in the sides of anti-pornography feminists. The latter can only accept that women engage in practices that appear to fly in the face of the 'loving relationship' image if they believe that these women do so against their will. (So pervasive is this 'victim' rationale that even sex offenders are 'explained' as having been abused in childhood, which conveniently pushes responsibility off into some distant past and distracts from the reality of contemporary, 'normal' families.) The 'victim' theory denies women the capacity voluntarily to step outside their allocated social roles. Those who swallow the victim label are rendered inert by self-pity; those who do not incite the wrath of their would-be redeemers.

Attacks on the sex industry are merely expressions of 'good woman/bad woman' attitudes. All those women who present themselves as 'respectable' are terrified of having the imaginary values they attach to themselves undercut by 'cheaper' women. Kate Millett claimed that prostitution is motivated either by economic need or 'a species of psychological addiction, built on self-hatred through the act of sale by which a whore is defined'.[1] Most people take up whoring because they consider it preferable to other forms of paid labour, much of which is certainly built upon employers' efforts to instil self-hatred in their staff. Underlying Millett's tirade are her 'good' woman's feelings of revulsion/fascination towards a woman who makes a blatant transaction out of what the former has been brought up to hold as sacred, dirty, and something to be engaged in only if the price is right (that is, if 'love' and emotional and economic security are offered in return).

Those feminists who weep crocodile tears over 'exploited' sex workers are doing nothing new. In the mid-nineteenth century, middle-class women in New York threatened to keep vigil outside brothels and to publish clients' names. They attacked low wages as a cause of prostitution and advocated better employment opportunities for women (perhaps in domestic service, where they might provide free sexual favours to the men of the house, who could then stop frittering away the family wealth in houses of ill-repute). In England in 1858 the Female Mission on the Fallen distributed tracts on the streets at night and opened rescue homes. The latest campaigns in this vein target sex tourism and mail-order brides. The poverty of third-world women was never of prime feminist concern until they became afraid that too many 'eligible' western men would be wrested from their grasp. The feminist who seeks a mate in lonely-hearts columns has to maintain the self-deception that her aims are all to do with romance and nothing to do with financial gain.

It is remarkable how sudden feelings of empathy and identification with 'exploited' women surge up in the breasts of feminists when they think of workers in the sex-industry – pornography is 'an assault on women, *our* dignity, *our* humanness, *our* personal safety, even our right to survive as autonomous individuals'.[2] It is even more remarkable how feminists never identify in this way with cleaners, child-minders and factory workers; that is, those 'hidden' women who create the material conditions that keep the feminist in the 'alternative' lifestyle to which she has become accustomed.

The argument that sex workers cause men to regard *all* women as sex objects is an expression of the latter-day Legion of Decency's fear of the lower orders. There is an unspoken assumption that working-class men are bound to translate their fantasies into practice. In 1891, 500 prominent women protested at the showing of two nudes in the Pennsylvania Academy of Fine Art. These days feminists do not seem to regard art galleries as breeding grounds for rapists; rather, it is the *Sun* or *Penthouse* reader who is spotlit as a potential sex attacker.

It is ludicrous to accuse a woman who poses naked in public of endangering other women. (Ironically, I once worked as an art model for a feminist who railed against page three girls for 'betraying' their sex.) Anti-pornography feminists are threatened by sex workers simply because they see them as not 'playing the game'. While pretending that the realms of love and sex are beyond economics, such feminists are holding out for the highest bidder. When Barbara Rogers complains that 'pornography [is] basically saying that all women are like prostitutes',[3] she is merely echoing the 'good' woman's fear that she might be seen to be as cheaply sexually available as she regards sex workers to be.

Those who wish to believe in a causal relationship between pornography and sexual violence can always drum up 'supporting evidence'. Pornography will, of course, be used in court as a 'contributory factor' in a case of sexual attack if it might serve to reduce the defendant's apparent responsibility for his crime.

If feminists believe that pornography causes violence against women, they must assume that its abolition would make life safer. Such naivety might best be corrected by a prolonged stay in a country where pornography is illegal, such as Saudi Arabia. I lived in Francoist Spain, where the incidence of rape and battery of women was in no way moderated by the stringent legal ban on pornography.

The Campaign Against Pornography & Censorship (CPC) tries to avoid identification with Mary Whitehouse and her ilk by suggesting that instead of banning pornography, victims of sexual violence should sue pornographers for causing their injuries, as doctors are sued for malpractice. If the CPC wish to entertain bizarre fantasies about the legal system then that is their business, but one might as well urge battered wives to take Mills & Boon to court on the grounds that romantic fiction caused them to believe in love and marriage.

Domestic violence is no more caused by *Woman's Own* or *The Virago Book of Love Poetry* than rape is by *Playboy*. Feminists tie themselves in knots trying to 'prove' the connection between pornography and sexual violence (the very existence of pornography is believed to constitute an act of violence against women). In reality, most women are beaten, raped and murdered by the men with whom they are 'in love'. Economic constraints, although highly important, are not the main reasons why women stay with or return to violent men. Women tolerate ill-treatment because they want to believe in the prevailing social fantasy of love as a recipe for earthly happiness. They are conditioned to reject any alternative prospects. My best friend declared at the age of 16 that, 'Life's not worth living if you don't get married.' Most women follow this credo to the point where they often put their own safety in jeopardy by turning a blind eye to anything that threatens to shatter their illusions. When I advised a friend in search of a man with whom to have children to check potential candidates for a history of violence (to themselves or others), she stared at me in despair: 'But that would hardly leave anyone.'

Anti-pornography feminists reinforce romantic illusions by portraying sexual fantasies outside a 'caring relationship between equals' as dangerous to women. As a result, they often find themselves in relationships with violent men. They use their politics as a signal to attract 'desirable' men (of the right accent and salary). Those males who pick up the message respond by coming across with apologies for the 'crimes' of their sex. Such anti-sexists are believed to make good mates. In my experience, the louder a man has proclaimed his good intentions towards womankind, the worse he has treated his partner. To give but two examples: I saw an anarchist on a Women Against Violence Against Women demonstration marching at the side of a woman he had attempted to strangle a couple of months previously; and a man who denounced domestic violence in a public meeting threatened me when I proceeded to publicize the fact that he had beaten up his girlfriend.

Unhappy personal experience seems to inspire increasingly wild delusions about the perfectability of love. The prevailing feminist fairy-tale is the 'equal' relationship: 'Of course non-patriarchal relationships do exist. A small minority of couples might even be termed egalitarian. The task is to make this type of relationship the predominant one.'[4] A few social adjustments are deemed necessary for the realization of the conjugal idyll. As long as the world knows that Daddy changes the nappies while Mummy works on her thesis, the real battles between the two can be played out away from public view. Preservation of a happy public face is vital if people are to believe in their own fantasies.

'Political lesbians' maintain that the romantic idyll can only ever be attained between women. Naturally, it took them a long time to acknowledge the incidence of lesbian battering which contradicts such wishful thinking. In fact, all the 'political dykes' I've ever known had male friends and lovers tucked away. Perhaps every would-be Dworkin has to have her Stoltenberg.[5] I heard one woman explain to a meeting that as a homosexual woman she could not have anything to do with heterosexual women, who might betray her by discussing her with *men*. I ran into her again a year later, by which time she had managed to produce a baby boy. It would seem that political dykedom is nothing but a ploy to keep other females away from 'eligible' men.

Lesbian sadomasochism sticks in the gullet of many feminists: 'Particularly in the light of patriarchal ideology which is premised on subordination, humiliation, and degradation of wimmin it is not OK for a womon to consent to her own humiliation.'[6] It is apparently 'OK' for a woman to get a job as a waitress or a secretary, however. Work is an exchange of degradation for money. I set my own limits. When I am asked to shave my legs, not to read during tea-break, or told not to argue with the boss, I quit. Anti-pornography feminists are quite comfortable with the degradation of the female (and male) labour force; many are employers themselves. They remain silent as millions of women wear out their mental and physical health – that is 'OK' so long as there are no topless calendars on the canteen walls. True to their puritan colours, they regard the sufferings of working women as ennobling, as 'proof' of female moral superiority (for women 'have to' work in the home as well, as the Wages For Housework Campaign reminded us). By contrast, such feminists go into frenzied outrage at women who parody conventional power relations and, worst of all, derive *pleasure* from doing so.

Anti-pornography feminists do their utmost to promote female fearfulness. They publicize male brutality to women as though it were the unique form of violence enacted in this world. It is portrayed as the greatest danger facing womankind and is supposed to generate an ever-present terror in the female psyche. According to Susan Brownmiller and company, the reign of 'sexual terrorism' constricts a woman's every thought and deed. If some men rape, then all men profit from the ensuing climate of fear that cows the female sex.[7] Pornography is presented as the terrorists' most effective weapon.

In response, feminists demand that society as a whole looks after them. They might sneer at Barbara Cartland's contention that men 'respond to an appeal from a weak creature in need of protection',[8] but essentially they believe this myth themselves. The implicit message, of safety through vulnerability, is broadcast by all those from Ms Cartland to Dworkin and MacKinnon who believe in the readiness of the 'decent chaps' in the government and police departments to protect them from the misogynist bad guys. This is naive in the extreme, for the agencies of the state are largely composed of men who ill-treat women, either directly or by means of the power granted them by their office. Only members of that class brought up to believe that the government exists for their benefit rather than their control could possibly entrust the state to decide what they may read or view.

Pro-censorship feminists, by looking to the state for protection, foster the same spirit of dependency that makes women vulnerable to violence in the first place. The main objective in bringing up a person as a woman is to convince her that she cannot survive without male protection. The brutalities committed against so many women by so many men who allegedly 'love' them is testament to the success of this indoctrination. Millions of women stay with the male 'protectors' who terrorize them because they have been so thoroughly convinced that the outside world holds even greater horrors. Protection is a euphemism for control. The more the wife relies upon her husband, or the feminist upon the state, the more autonomy she surrenders and the more vulnerable she becomes.

Some feminists demand that anything they find offensive be removed from 'women's space'; for example, they propose that 'men's magazines' be taken out of the newsagents and confined to special sex shops. Presumably the latter are 'off-limits' to women. The logical extension of this argument is the gender apartheid of segregated train compartments and purdah. I, personally, shall continue to use the 'Gents' when the queue for the 'Ladies' is too long.

Anti-pornography campaigners do not simply aim for a topographical separation of the sexes. Their portrayal of 'inherent' gender differences is more fantastical than anything Barbara Cartland or D.H. Lawrence have produced. The infinite nobility of the female soul is contrasted with the brutishness of men. This extends from personal relationships to international politics. The 'women's peace movement' urges the angel to fly out of the house on a mission to rid the world of war and every other sort of nastiness. During the Falklands War I was informed by feminists that Margaret Thatcher is a man. They had worked this out as the only explanation for her patent failure to conform to the feminine stereotype.

Ultimately, the campaign against pornography is self-defeating in its declared intent to reduce the amount of violence inflicted on women by men. As a political strategy it serves to intensify female vulnerability. Not only does it encourage women to depend on others, it exhorts them to concentrate on changing men and society, rather than to question their own motives for tolerating ill-treatment. Preoccupation with others rather than the self has traditionally been deemed an essential attribute of 'womanliness'. The campaign reinforces the ideals of female passivity and self-sacrifice that have long encouraged women to bear ill-treatment. The striving to 'rescue' others through the power of love and understanding is the life-work of millions of women. Wives who believe they can 'reform' the men who abuse them remain locked in their miserable lives. Such futility is matched by those feminists who so desperately want the male sex to live up to romantic mythology.

11

The Anti-sexism Campaign Invites you to Fight Sexism, Not Sex

CHRISTOBEL MACKENZIE

The Anti-Sexism Campaign was formed because we felt no one was really taking a broad feminist approach to women's issues. We had hoped some of the new groups that have formed over the last couple of years would be taking on those issues, but they all seem to be very tame and afraid to challenge some of the basic assumptions of sexist society. We also felt that it was time a group that encompassed all sexes and sexualities worked together for sexual liberation from a feminist perspective. It seems to us that groups based on a single identity – for example black women, lesbian, gay, or even women's groups – tend to work from just one point of view, ignore other issues of sexism, and stereotype people who do not share their identity.

One issue in which we found a shocking lack of interest was ageism. We thought this was an obvious issue for women, since society always slows us down in making decisions about our lives, and many women are much older when they get into the workforce, so discrimination against older people is a real problem in getting economic equality for women. It's harder for women to get jobs if we aren't considered 'attractive', and we all know that for a woman to be seen as attractive, she must be young. The kind of self-confidence and capability that only come with experience isn't really appreciated in women – if we are young, we are easier to push around, aren't we? If we are insecure, it's easier to get us to do things that aren't in our job descriptions, too. And if we want to have children, we get pushed even further down the job ladder – no one thinks experience in raising children and running a home is a 'real' skill, so if we enter the workforce after raising children, we are seen as not having 'worked' and are harder to employ. And we are older, so less 'desirable'.

Ageism is a problem for the young, too. Adults think that being paternalistic – 'protecting' us from knowing and doing things – is a way to avoid sullying our 'innocence'. This is hard on us all, but particularly for young females, who are seen as *more* vulnerable and 'innocent' than young males. Sometimes this 'protection' can lead to harsh treatment for girls who are doing things that are seen as 'natural' for boys – girls who express their sexuality early can find themselves being treated like criminals, even though boys don't usually have this problem unless they're expressing gay sexuality. But all children are under pressure to act out the 'innocent child' role when it comes to sex – we are supposed to pretend that we don't have sexual feelings and can't want sexual interactions – and we all get punished for anything that shows adults that we aren't so 'innocent'.

We wonder why feminists still accept the idea of 'innocence' when we are really talking about sexual *ignorance*. Why is this still treated like a virtue? Sex isn't something that should be seen as blameworthy in the first place, so why do we keep talking about it in terms of innocence, when the opposite, obviously, is guilt and blame? Having sexual feelings or sexual experience does not mean you have bad thoughts or do bad things. When we accept lies like this, we let the world create other lies – we are ashamed to admit to sexuality, so we pretend we don't have sexual feelings, and the adult world can go on pretending that children are not sexual at all. How else can 'experts' still claim that people don't have orgasms before they reach puberty, when we know women who have masturbated to orgasm when they were only five years old? How else can people think that children and teenagers won't learn to be sexual unless they take sex education classes or see pornography, when we know women who discovered masturbation all by themselves before they had ever heard about any kind of sex at all? And boys are certainly both sexual and sexist before they ever see pornography or get sex education.

Of course, these lies go on for women even into adulthood. We aren't supposed to be really sexual, and we are discouraged from admitting we have positive feelings about being sexual. We are somehow seen as 'dirty' or 'bad' if we have sexual experience or if we admit we like sex. We are so afraid to be seen as 'whores' that we accept the idea of ourselves as 'victims' if we have sex. All this does for women is make being a victim seem natural. If a woman can't admit she has sex because she wants sex, then of course she is having sex in exchange for something else, whether it's love, marriage, status, the security of a home for herself and her children, or just plain money. How can so many feminists look down on prostitutes when whoring is really the only form of sexual expression that is considered acceptable for women? If we don't really like sex, that means we are always doing it in exchange for something else – always whoring. Yet the only women who *can't* be accused of prostituting themselves sexually – the ones who have sex only because they really want to do it – are the ones who are most likely to be called 'whores'. Is this sexist society's way of trying to keep women sexually repressed?

Why is 'whore' such a dirty word, anyway? We all know that, no matter what our jobs are, we are supposed to behave differently from men in the workplace, and we are defined by our gender in terms of both what jobs we are encouraged to get into and how we are supposed to do the jobs we are in. 'Women's jobs' always seem to carry expectations that we will add a 'woman's touch' to the workplace, on behalf of men. Why is a woman who types on a computer a 'secretary' when a man who does it is a 'word-processor'? Why is a male receptionist a 'security officer' and why is he paid so much more than a female receptionist? Why is it that female office juniors, typists, and receptionists are usually expected to make coffee when men in the same jobs are not? Why is it that even when women have 'men's' jobs, we are still expected to do more fetching and carrying and service-type errands than the men in those jobs? And why are women expected to dress in feminine clothes, 'show some leg', and wear flimsy (and sometimes dangerous) shoes in so many jobs that we are told are not part of the sex industry? And even where we aren't made to feel like decorations, many jobs can be boring, repetitive, gruelling and dangerous. Why pretend sex work can't be a legitimate choice over many 'respectable' jobs?

The fact is that *most* women are expected to sell sex in one way or another, flatter male egos and soften male lives, whatever our jobs are. Prostitutes are at least allowed the dignity of not having to pretend they are doing something else. No other female-defined job offers the potential for as much freedom and choice in terms of who you work for, when you work, and what you do, as well as the time you spend doing it – and we believe that it is the freedom of prostitutes that is the real threat to patriarchal society, and the reason it is so easy to get just about everyone (including feminists) to jump on the bandwagon of condemning women who trade sex for money. The 'evil' that prostitutes do is to strip away the illusion that women do not sell sex – in the workplace, in marriage, or on the street. Hookers 'blow our cover' – they tell the world the truth. That's the real reason why 'respectable' women hate them.

And 'respectable' women (again, including feminists), hate the women who say they like sex – especially the women who like sex with men. If women like sex, then we are not always the perfect victims of violent or coercive males. If women like sex, then sex isn't the 'price' of the things women 'get' from men (home, marriage, love, security, etc.). Most of all, if some women like sex, then the women who have only endured sex for the sake of their relationships have been lying to themselves, selling themselves for no good reason. The patriarchy has a great deal to fear from the women who like sex, which is why they always find more nasty words to call us – whores, dykes, sluts, nymphomaniacs – to keep us in our place.

But, then, why should 'dyke' be a dirty word, either? There was a time, of course, when it was easy to dismiss lesbians as 'sad' women who were either just 'sick' or, even more unfortunately, couldn't find men to love them. As long as lesbianism was seen only as a sexless alliance between women who needed a substitute for 'real' relationships with men, society tended for the most part to ignore dykes. No one could think they were actually being sexual, anyway. Lesbianism was not equated with independence so much as with failure, in those days.

But gay liberation and the women's movement have in some part changed that, and today lesbians are seen as much more sexual. People no longer assume that dykes don't have sexual lives and really just 'need a man'. The result, in straight society, is that lesbianism is seen as much more threatening. Lesbianism is the ultimate denial of the theory that sex is just something women have to do for men, that it is not something we can like for ourselves. After all, if we are doing it with each other, that means that no man is forcing us to do it – we aren't 'victims' after all! And it also means that there is no 'price' for relationships. Could this mean that women and men might have interactions in which we trade sex directly for sex, and love directly for love, just as lesbians do? That would make us truly equal – and completely upset the patriarchal economy between women and men.

So it's not surprising that lesbians who are seen as enjoying sex are just as frightening as straight women who enjoy sex. These are the 'bad' lesbians, and even in fairly liberal circles they are looked down on. Straight people who are perfectly willing to accept lesbians who they perceive as having nice little sexless relationships are still horrified by lesbians who like sex – *those* women are really letting the side down, having sex when they don't even 'have to'! But those 'dirty' lesbians are paying a price in a new kind of repression that is being placed on them by anti-sex feminists.

Many feminists seem to expect lesbians to provide an image of women as 'nice' and 'pure' – as if the existence of lesbian culture should serve as a continual reminder to society that women don't really like sex, that we are 'above' sex and aloof from it. This is particularly scary because that is exactly the image many rapists have of women, and they use it as an excuse for what they do – because we are above them and above sex, we are not really touched by any of it, whether we do it as hookers, 'for love', or whether it is forced on us by rapists.

It's frightening to see so many feminists who want so desperately to believe that women can't enjoy sex, that every time we have sex with men, we are being victims. Why is it so necessary to see ourselves as poor little put-upon sufferers? Why do we need to think that when men want to be with us, they only want to 'take advantage' of us? Why must we always treat male sexuality as violent, opportunistic and evil? Why can't we admit that men, too, want love and relationships? It's certainly no accident that straight society always enjoys making the 'point', however false it may be, that lesbian relationships are always sexless and gay male relationships never last.

In fact, all unconventional relationships are constantly under attack; everywhere you go, people are quick to tell you that 'those kinds of relationship never last', and if your unusual relationship does show signs of lasting, a whole of range people, your parents and even your friends, will be working hard to make it as difficult as possible. What no one wants to acknowledge is that *most* relationships don't last. How many of us have started relationships that were completely conventional in our own cultures (whether lesbian, gay male, or straight), with the approval of all, only to have them fall apart after a few weeks or months? How many of us feel utter amazement that we have reached the five-year mark in a relationship, for the first time, after having had one false start after another? And how many of the relationships that *do* work can honestly be called 'normal'?

The most unusual, unacceptable relationships of all between adults are, of course, the non-monogamous ones. One of the things that makes it easy for straight society to claim that gay relationships don't work is that we equate active monogamy (where the partners do have sex with each other, but with no one else) with 'successful' relationships. If you are sexual with someone other than your partner, then your relationship with your partner isn't 'real' – obviously, if you want sex with someone else, you can't love your partner. We also assume that 'real' partnerships are sexual, so that if partners don't actually have sex with each other, this too is a failed relationship. For many people, this turns sex into a battleground where they must constantly be initiating or submitting to sex to 'prove' their love, rather than because they want to have sex. For others, the validity of the relationship is in constant question just because other people might turn them, or their partners, on.

It is astonishing that even many feminists accept monogamy as the goal. As much as we recognize male jealousy as an intrusion on female independence, we still allow ourselves to feel betrayed by lovers who have sexual interests in other people, or by men who just want to look at nude photos of other women! What can this possibly have to do with the real relationships people have? Why should we feel like our lives are being destroyed just because we aren't all things to our partners? No one can do this, and the pressure on women to be 'all things' to 'our men' (usually, our husbands) was always one of the most oppressive things in our lives – we were kept constantly chained to this full-time occupation at which no one could possibly succeed, and had no time to think of ourselves. Why should we try to impose this same scheme of trying to be each others' exclusive property on other people any longer? Why do even lesbian feminists get caught up on the idealization of monogamy? If we keep treating our partners' sexuality as property, we should not be surprised when society keeps treating all female sexuality as the property of men.

And it must be remembered that being a 'couple' is no more desirable than other parts of sexism – couplism is another kind of sexuality that is just a forced institution in this society, much like heterosexism. People should be free to form couples or not, have multiple relationships or no relationships, without being shoe-horned into ways of living that don't necessarily suit us. Being a couple can be a straitjacket, and society doesn't make room for people who are not, or don't want to be, in a couple, which makes it even more oppressive.

Channelling sexuality into monogamous marriage serves the needs of the state in controlling both women and men, but particularly women. It keeps women tied to the home and children, with the children supervised and repressed by their parents. It also makes men feel chained to hateful jobs that they must keep without complaint for fear of threatening their families' security, and strips them of their humanistic connections to others so that they can be shunted into jobs that damage the environment or even kill people – whether in industry or as soldiers – without allowing them to feel grief, guilt or rebellion. Gay men, of course, represent a threat to employers in that they often have no such familial constraints to force them to accept this kind of oppression on the job. Gay men who have families have a double bind on them – they still care about the security of their children and even their wives, and they have the further threat of not being able to find new jobs if they are known to be gay. These same fears also keep parents from making waves socially or politically, including even fairly mild community activism – if your face gets into the local newspaper, your children may suffer; if you are gay as well, you can't afford to call attention to yourself for fear the authorities may take reprisals by interfering in your home, even taking away your children.

We can't waste any more time arguing over symptoms of sexism and attacking the wrong targets – like sexual fantasy, pornography or bisexuality. We should stop trying to screw each other into acceptable roles and begin to admit that we are all different, and that is no bad thing. Liberation means welcoming diversity and celebrating pleasure, at last.

12

The Wages of Anti-censorship Campaigning

FEMINISTS AGAINST CENSORSHIP

Feminists Against Censorship (FAC) was formed in the spring of 1989 by and for feminist women who wanted to campaign for free expression – particularly on sexual issues – from a feminist perspective. It was immediately made clear to us that anti-pornography campaigners were unprepared to accept the possibility that any woman who had a feminist understanding of their view of pornography could possibly disagree with it, and we became the victims of one spurious accusation after another.

On our first appearance, we were asked where we got all our money – the implication being that we had a great deal of it. In fact, we had collected £100 from among our members in order to produce our first leaflet, and had no other funds; but in short order we heard that we were 'known to be heavily funded' – usually by 'the multi-million dollar American porn industry'. The presence of several North American women at our group's first appearance was frequently cited as 'evidence' that we were obviously connected with American pornographers. (We had three at that action: one Canadian student, one visiting lover of a British group member, and one Canadian woman who had already lived and worked here for many years in the movement. All three women are feminist activists and lesbians; none of them had anything to do with the porn industry.)

Given the astonishing bigotry of this accusation, it was all the more incomprehensible when we were accused of being *racist* – not because of anything we actually did or said, but simply because we opposed censorship of pornography. We were told that pornography was racist, and therefore we could not defend it without also being racist. We thought this was a curious charge to begin with, since most visual media are at least as racist – non-white women are not portrayed as being attractive in the same way that white women are (or as often) in most television and film. But then we found out that the charge of racism in this case was based not only on the low number of 'women of colour' in the porn industry, but also on their presence – if pornography features

146

black women, that too is racist. (Similarly, pornography is 'able-ist' when there are only able-bodied women in its pictures, but is 'fetishizing deformity' when amputees appear.) These interpretations did not take the sting out of being accused of racism by women who were being blatantly racist themselves.

Despite the fact that the largest donation we have ever received was £50, we have been dogged right into the present by rumours of our alleged large-scale funding. Sometimes it takes more subtle forms: after a recent public meeting of Campaign Against Pornography, we received a letter from an attendee who wanted to know how we 'answer their charge' that we are a group composed entirely of 'rich upper-class women'. One or two of the original members of the group may have come from more comfortable families, but most of us did not; quite a few of us come from economically disadvantaged backgrounds, and even those of us from the middle class have found it difficult to support ourselves in a sexist environment where unemployment has been virtually normalized. A few of our members are successful academics, but far more of us work at ordinary jobs, or in marginal work, and many are unemployed. The only requirement for a member or supporter of Feminists Against Censorship is a willingness to oppose censorship from a feminist perspective, and quite a few women with no money do support our goals – and we welcome them. However, if any rich women would like to send us money, we wouldn't turn it down; we have looked in vain for a sugar momma.

Of course, we found the charge that we are 'rich upper-class women' doubly ironic for other reasons. The feminist movement has pointed out for years that coming from a wealthy background does not necessarily protect a woman from the oppressions of sexism: women who have wealthy fathers or husbands quickly discover that the money is not their own, and some research has shown that working-class women, because their husbands don't have *much* more money than they do, also have more power in relation to their husbands than do the wives of rich or 'professional' men. The person most likely to rape an upper-class white woman is an upper-class white man – the very sort of man who is least likely ever to be convicted of the crime. Domestic violence is hardly limited to the lower economic classes, and having your efforts treated as trivial merely because you are female is a problem that cuts across class, as feminists continue to point out. 'You have more in common with your maid than you do with your husband', was how Gloria Steinem used to phrase it. Are we now being told that rich, upper-class women can not possibly have any legitimate experience or concern with regard to gender issues?

A more interesting point is that many 'feminist' criticisms of the sex industry seem to rest with the belief, held principally by middle- and upper-class women, that all other jobs available to women are necessarily better than those in the sex industry. The working-class women who make up a substantial part of the sex industry are not deeply moved by the suggestion that being pushed around and demoralized for 40 hours a week is so much better than posing for pornography for a few hours and making a lot more money at it. Nor are they thrilled to hear that feminists want to make them criminals and throw them in jail. Do anti-pornography feminists really imagine that sexual harassment happens *only* in relation to porn, or never occurs in any other industry? Do they think that working in a factory, or standing at a counter, is so much more desirable than being a 'page three' girl? Many anti-pornography feminists, coming from comfortable middle-class backgrounds themselves, have never had to think about the options working-class women are often trying to avoid by going into porn; work as a housewife in a mining town, or a bar maid, or a waitress, or on an assembly line, are not positions that are devoid of sexism, abuse and harassment.

But this is only one example of how class issues pervade the pornography debates. The distinctions between (acceptable) erotica and (unacceptable) pornography are obviously class based, as is the presumption of women who consider themselves sophisticated and therefore believe they are entitled to tell others what they 'should' want to do with their lives, or to protect working-class people from material that might 'deprave and corrupt' them. When *The Late Show* held a round-table discussion of the Brett Easton Ellis book *An American Psycho*, a female member of the panel stated that men would read the erotic parts and become aroused, then be unable to damp that arousal when the erotic scenes were followed by violence – and thereby learn to eroticize violence themselves. Author Iain Banks, also present, said that, on the contrary, he was turned on by the 'sexy bits' and, when he got to the violent bits, was turned off, to which the woman replied, 'Yes, but you're *sophisticated*' – in other words, it's just the 'lower orders' who have to be protected from books. Anti-porn campaigner Moyra Bremner says she is worried that 'girls' will pick up a book by de Sade thinking it's Mills & Boon, and that 'truck drivers' will read de Sade and get ideas. Deliver us from 'sophisticated' people who want to 'protect' the working classes.

Irony is heaped on irony; Andrea Dworkin was given an hour to herself on television to explain her anti-porn position – no opposing voice was needed, it was said, because Ms Dworkin explained *our* view for us well enough. No equally one-sided hour has been offered to anti-censorship feminists, of course. Yet Dworkin and her friends and colleagues all complain that *their* view is being suppressed: Barbara Rogers falsely suggests (in *Pornography and Sexual Violence: Evidence of the Links*) that the evidence against pornography cannot find a publisher because the publishing companies are engaged in a conspiracy of silence on the issue; Ms Dworkin claims her books are suppressed, and so on. In fact, most authors would dearly love to have been published as 'few' times as Andrea Dworkin, and the material to which Barbara Rogers refers is available far more cheaply through non-commercial means. Labour MP Clare Short, who is listened to by some because she is believed to be feminist, was once offered the opportunity to appear with a FAC member on Gloria Hunniford's show; she refused, she said, to be on 'with some vituperative feminist,' and we were dropped from the show. Strangely, she has not objected to being placed opposite the managing editor of UK *Penthouse*, Isabel Kaprowski – such women can be dismissed as having no opinions of their own, thanks to the patronizing image anti-porn women have drawn of them. When Feminists Against Censorship made our objections on *Right to Reply* to a one-sided anti-pornography episode of *Dispatches*, we received letters, as we so often do, from women who were surprised to hear that there was any feminist group opposing censorship. This is the natural result of the fact that the anti-pornography view has received so much more publicity than ours has; we can only hope some day to be 'suppressed' as much as they.

Meanwhile, as more women hear of us, more women are questioning the anti-porn position. Some of them join FAC. Not unnaturally, women who work in the sex industry sometimes contact us and join. Although we originally had no contact with the porn industry, we have now discovered that women who work in it are often feminists themselves, and are delighted to find, at last, the one feminist group where they won't be treated like scum and continually asked to apologize for or lie about who and what they are. The fact that women who work for sex magazines have developed a relationship with FAC has, of course, now been used against us as 'proof' of our links to the porn industry. The final irony is that the owners of British porn magazines have given us no support from the top; they permit the women who work for them to express their own views in public and to join our group, and that is the extent of it. FAC wants the abolition of the Obscene Publications Act; this would create competition for the soft-porn publishers that they are not prepared to meet, so they have no interest in supporting us. Campaign Against Pornography have received funding for a paid worker; we have no such luxuries.

So, you get accused of every evil under the sun, dismissed as an intellect and as a feminist, and credited with having comfortable resources you don't have. Still, we think it's important to remind women that sexism is not as simple as pictures of sex, and censorship is bound to do us more harm than good, so we keep on doing it anyway, even though it most often leaves us out of pocket.

You don't get much from being an anti-censorship activist – but we think you should, all the same. Join us: Feminists Against Censorship, BM Box 207, London WC1N 3XX.

Conclusion: Women Still Want Freedom

ALISON ASSITER AND AVEDON CAROL

Over the last several years, the focal issue for feminists in the British Isles has been the question of pornography: what is it, and can we – or should we – 'do something' about it? Sexually explicit material seems to symbolize women's exclusion from male society – the feeling that men quite deliberately use sex as a means to lord it over us, make us feel put-down and left out. Yet many women know that censorship – that favourite tool of fascists – is too dangerous to embrace, and that the problems between men and women go far deeper than mere pictures of sexual acts. Often, we find that women who deplore the excesses of pornography still cannot accept censorship as a means to deal with it. They seek a balance where we can reduce unconsenting exposure to sexual material without giving the government further power to choose our entertainments and reading material for us. Other women see positive qualities, or potential, in sexually explicit material, and want to see it changed to reflect our experience and interest so that it can benefit us all.

The critical analysis of films, books, art and magazines, in order to expose their sexist content, is a long-standing feminist practice. One of the earliest and most valued works of feminist critical theory is Kate Millet's *Sexual Politics*.[1] In that book, she graphically illustrated the blatant sexism of the 'male-defined' view of women's sexuality in the works of popular, yet relatively 'highbrow', male writers like Henry Miller and Norman Mailer. But, far from calling for censorship of such texts, she suggested ways of reading them that brought the androcentric context to the fore. Since then, a whole genre of feminist critical theory of this kind has flourished, where the texts of male writers as diverse as Shakespeare and Ian Fleming have been analysed to reveal their sexism. Many feminists recognize that a call for censorship of androcentric texts would cover most of our cultural history, and they would be unwilling to take such a drastic step. As Gayle Rubin has pointed out, feminists have for many years criticized sexism in the media, but we never called for any particular form or genre to be banned.[2] There is no reason to do so now.

Many anti-porn feminists seem to feel that there is no middle ground between a ban on pornography and open, uncritical acceptance of it. But criticism is necessary to any genre; it feeds an entire industry of editors, critics, reviewers and publishers of reviews. Pornography has suffered less detailed, public criticism of this sort, because it is an underground genre. But that doesn't mean there *is* no criticism within the industry or among its consumers, nor that it can't or hasn't benefited by such criticism. Unfortunately, when an entire genre is written off by 'serious' critics, the details of what may be wrong with it go largely unexamined (as do its virtues). Still, when art, however wrong-headed it may be in its experimental focus, is examined in the light, more opportunities exist for it to improve, broaden and break the boundaries of its genre-defined limits. This happened with science fiction, once a much maligned category most noted for its stereotypical cardboard characters, now seen as a source of some of our finest modern fiction.

Criticism has always been an important part of free speech. It is, in many respects, what free speech is *about*. No social activist would ever consent to leaving the disturbing or problematic features of society unremarked; every feminist is, in her way, a critic of male supremacist culture. This holds true for pornography as with everything else; and, as with every other genre, criticism of pornography must not be equated with a reason to censor it. Sexual material is not a special case.

It is important for women to remember that sex isn't the *only* area where sexism manifests itself – it's just the one that is most obvious, because women have been taught to be particularly sensitive to it. If we look at the horror stories women tell about the means by which employers, co-workers and lovers have used sex oppressively, we can find parallels outside the sexual arena: for each husband who tells his spouse she is a 'bad wife' because she doesn't live up to his sexual expectations, there is another husband who offers the same abuse to a wife who doesn't cook or keep house like his mother did; for every group of men who use pornography or talk about sex as a means of making female friends and co-workers feel like they 'don't belong there', there are men who talk about sports or electronics in a way that makes women feel excluded.

Similarly, when Campaign Against Pornography members talk about third-world sex workers who died when the building they were locked into burned down, they are saying nothing that didn't once happen in the garment industry to women who were locked into their place of work. But when the 'ladies' who made clothing died, no one said the garment industry should be closed down; rather, the rights and safety of female workers were the issue.[3] Illegality and stigmatization play the greatest role in making the sex industry unsafe for women; we will never protect women from the sex industry's excesses by driving it further underground.

Women who were involved in the fight for racial equality and the anti-war protests of the 1960s are all too well aware of the true nature of censorship – it is a tool that can be used by those in power whenever they want to suppress the free exchange of knowledge and ideas. Those who remember the *Oz* trail know that the editors were put on trial for political reasons, and not merely for sexual indecency. Decades earlier, Margaret Sanger was arrested for 'obscenity' when she told women in the United States about birth control, and, as Tom Robinson said in 'Glad to Be Gay':

> There's no nudes in *Gay News*, our one magazine
> But they still find excuses to call it 'obscene'.

In other words, if you give them one excuse to censor something, they'll use it to censor *you* – especially if you are someone who is willing to stand up to sexism.

And standing up to sexism *must* mean a great deal more than merely attacking pornography. When numerous magazines promote the ideal of woman-as-housewife (such as *Woman's Own*), or encourage women to undertake life-threatening diets in order to become dangerously thin, pornography is hardly the worst of our enemies.[4]

The women who contributed to this book expressed a strong sense that feminists have led themselves down the garden path to accepting yet more sexism. By attacking sexuality itself rather than sexual mythology and repression, they feel, we've actually made the problem worse for ourselves. Many feminists seem to think that getting away from oppression means getting away from sex, but it's interesting to hear from women like Tuppy Owens or Annie Sprinkle,[5] who stepped outside of the dominant culture altogether, embraced the sex industry, and felt a sense of empowerment that we 'respectable' women seldom experience. How is it that these women who have pursued sexuality so openly have managed to escape the horrors the rest of us thought were unavoidable anywhere?

Of course, in the dominant culture, women are so aware of being judged sexually in inappropriate circumstances that we feel we must go out of our way to suppress any sexual thought or expression. Indeed, it is our job to suppress such thoughts – our roles as women, defined in reproductive terms, demand that we forever control the fabric of social interaction, the stability of the family, the behaviour of men. (In the old, traditional social model, women were expected to channel male sexuality towards the home in order to protect the stability of society and the family; the new, 'politically correct' model instructs women to focus our sexual behaviour on the destruction of patriarchy. Both models treat female sexuality as no more than a tool for social construction.)

But didn't we get into feminism because we were sick of being defined by our reproductive capacity, exhausted from trying to control men and set the sexual limits? Weren't we hoping for the same right men have to relax, lose control once in a while, drop our guard now and then without having to pay a life-long price? Didn't we demand to know why both social rules and legislative restrictions governing sexuality *and employment* centralized reproduction, as if it was the only thing we ever did? (Why else were men better able to get jobs, and given bigger pay packets than women?)

It's interesting to see how feminist argument has moved away from talking about reproduction as being central to sexism. In the early 1970s, feminists devoted enormous resources to discussing women's oppression in terms of our child-bearing and child-rearing role, and although Shulamith Firestone's talk of artificial wombs may seem a bit over the top (and overly technologically based) now, we all acknowledged that she had located the problem correctly. Nowadays, Andrea Dworkin and Sheila Jeffreys both seem to place intercourse and the phallus at the centre of oppression, as if reproduction and child-care had nothing to do with it.

But reproduction has *everything* to do with it. Andrea Dworkin is right when she complains that we treat heterosexual intercourse – the mating of reproductive organs – as central to sex. It's no accident that only male arousal and satisfaction really count in 'sex' when only men are required to come to arousal in order to reproduce.

This explains society's downright fetishistic resistance to any sexuality that doesn't ultimately lead to heterosexual intercourse:

masturbation is not something one should admit to, although manual manipulation is acceptable as 'foreplay' between partners as long as male orgasm takes place during copulation; oral sex is revolting on its own, but sometimes justifiable if it facilitates intercourse; anal intercourse is still treated as generally taboo; fantasy sexuality, like SM, which often ignores intercourse altogether, is treated as an outrageous perversion; homosexual couples are 'pretended families' who might be tolerated in some liberal circles if they manage to ape reproductive pairings well enough to convince us that they *respect* the institutions, even if they can't perfect them.

The degree to which you are 'liberal' about sex can be defined by the degree to which you accept the aforementioned sexual variations as tolerable: the moral right wants you to cut straight to intercourse – in heterosexual marriage and for procreative purposes only, with no birth control – and everything else is 'perversion'; progressives admit that sex can be fun and, actually, it isn't usually done for reproductive purposes anyway, so as long as you do it within certain limits that still acknowledge reproductive potential, you're all right; 'respectable' homosexuals sneer at the non-monogamous and those who wear leather; and a small number of sex radicals, voices in the wilderness, continue to insist that mutuality and consent (and safer sex, please!) are the truly important rules.

The fatal mistake of the anti-sex feminists has been the assumption that society designs our sexual interactions with the sexual service of men by women as the end goal. Both Dworkin and Jeffreys seem to believe that the purpose of heterosexism and sexism in general is a male conspiracy to get women to provide the maximum amount of sexual pleasure to males – but this hardly explains why society deliberately limits female willingness to become involved in sex, nor why fellatio, male voyeurism, female exhibitionism, 'hand jobs' and the like are stigmatized. (If Jeffreys is correct, why aren't girls trained from birth to suck cock?) No, it's clear that our society has fetishized reproduction to the point that even where sex is clearly undertaken when conception is not desired, we still fear to acknowledge outright that we're not in it for the babies. Our whole society continues to make room only for sex that appears to be directed at some version of a nuclear family. *This* is the focus that feminists should be taking on again.

Recently, we've seen signs of a new season for feminism, just as the government is catching up to ideas that we discarded years ago. While both the Tories and Labour make new calls for sexual censorship, women are saying they have something else in mind. More women are saying outright that consent and openness are important, that repression is the wrong way to go. The gay community is no longer so harshly anti-bisexual, and the 'no leather' rules have disappeared from gay venues.[6] Transsexuals are welcomed without animosity where once they were banned. Lesbians in Britain are even making their own home-grown pornography for women, and quite a few heterosexual women have become involved in creating pornographic materials aimed at a female audience. (Why, men are even beginning to take condoms seriously.) Yet the authorities, in anticipation of the trade barriers coming down, have already been more censorious than ever in recent years, claiming they intend to stem a tide of 'foreign filth' from Europe. They even confiscate safe sex posters – this in the midst of a tragic health crisis. And the clubs where SM dykes and body-art fanciers hang out have suffered the loss of one venue after another under police pressure. There is more than one kind of bigotry at work here, and feminists should want no part of this excuse for nationalistic fascism.

Those of us who still want liberation for women are not interested in having the government snoop into our bedrooms. We want to talk about the sexism that affects us in hiring and on the job and still leaves us with considerably smaller incomes than men have. We want to know what is *really* at the root of sexual violence, and how to fight it. We want to know if men have a place in our lives and if we are ever going to be happy on the same planet together. We want to know if there really is such a thing as 'sisterhood' or if this is just another guilt-trip to keep us in line. We want a chance to find out what our real potential is – in intellectual fields, in physical endeavour, and sexually. Most of all, we want the same thing we wanted all along – to be respected as the multi-faceted individuals we are, and not to be squeezed into more ill-fitting stereotypes.

Notes and References

Introduction

1. William Morrow & Company, Inc., New York, 1970. Although a great deal of important work has always originated in Britain, we will often refer to US works and experience, both because they have generated so many more quotes, and because so much of the rhetoric that filtered into the general discourse in the UK originated in North America. This is particularly notable in the anti-pornography movement, where statistics and analyses that refer only to US media and law are frequently repeated by anti-pornography feminists here as if they were also true for Britain.

2. Woodhull was one of the truly outrageous women among earlier feminists. As Lisa Tuttle put it in her *Encyclopedia of Feminism* (Longman, 1986): 'In 1871, she scored a great victory for the suffrage movement by convincing the Senate Judiciary Committee to hear her plea for a constitutional amendment; in the same year, however, she scandalized the more conservative suffragists by speaking in favour of free love, and was defeated in her bid for leadership of the National Woman Suffrage Association. Undeterred, she ran for President of the United States, the first woman ever to do so.'

3. Cultural feminism is the belief that what once were called 'feminine' traits – nurturance rather than competitiveness, diffidence rather than assertiveness, and so on – are the natural behaviour of women; that men and women differ radically in thought patterns, talents, preferences and sexuality; and that this dualism should be enforced and made central to any social structuring. This used to be known as 'sexism'. For an invaluable discussion of the degeneration of radical feminism into cultural feminism, see 'The Taming of the Id: Feminist Sexual Politics, 1968–1983' by Alice Echols in Carole S. Vance (ed.) *Pleasure and Danger*, Routledge and Kegan Paul, Boston, London, Melbourne and Henley, 1984.

4. Essentially, political lesbianism is a conscious choice to relate only to other women, based not on erotic preference, but on

157

the exclusion of men from our relationships. Many women saw this as the only way forward because they felt that relationships with men were just too problematic.

5. It should be kept in mind, however, that heterosexual feminists did not always behave well toward lesbians in the early days, either. Many straight women were horrified to see their movement equated with sexual deviance and did their best to keep the lesbians within the movement invisible. Heterosexual feminists were understandably irate when men responded to them with irrelevant charges of 'lesbianism', but lesbians were equally justified in their anger at being told to suppress their own authentic voice.

6. This refusal to acknowledge the possible joys of heterosexual involvement played an important role in alienating black women from the feminist movement in the United States, as well. Black feminists tended to be older and, therefore, more sexually experienced than many white feminists, and their insistence that sex with men was not always a painful and demeaning experience was met with blank incomprehension and denial by white middle-class feminists. White women often tended to assume that some peculiarity of social dysfunction in the black community made it difficult for black women to understand why they shouldn't like sex; black women frequently expressed the view that there was something deeply wrong with whites if this was how white women perceived sex.

7. See Sheila Jeffreys in *Anticlimax* and Janice Raymond's *The Transsexual Empire* for particularly reactionary and anti-human approaches to transsexuals.

8. The term 'radical feminism' originally referred to the belief that sexism is a fundamental oppression (radical = going to the root). However, many people today mistakenly hold the belief that a 'radical feminist' is indistinguishable from a lesbian separatist or political lesbian. Yet there are still quite a few radical feminists who believe that political lesbianism itself is a diversion which fails to address the roots of sexism.

9. Long hair on men was seen as breaking down gender roles – long-haired males were accused of looking 'like girls', suspended from schools, and sometimes even physically attacked in the streets.

10. See 'The Primarolo Bill' in this volume for a version of the Dworkin-MacKinnon definition of 'pornography'. Dworkin-MacKinnon seeks to evade the constitutional ban on

censorship by re-defining pornography as a civil rights violation.

11. Carole Vance points out that in the Meese Commission hearings on pornography, the term 'degrading to women' was converted by right-wing panel members to 'degrading to femininity' – a very different concept indeed, but right in line with the right-wing opposition to feminism that was made so dramatically clear at the 1992 Republican Party Convention. See 'Negotiating Sex and Gender in the Attorney General's Commission on Pornography' in Lynne Segal and Mary McIntosh (eds.) *Sex Exposed*, Virago, 1992.

12. Indeed, the right have lately taken to implying that child abuse is a relatively new phenomenon, that it is 'spreading' because of divorce (putting children in contact with step-fathers who feel unrestrained by the incest taboo), pornography, gay rights, and so on. But this is entirely false; it has been with us for quite a long time. Freud was so shocked by the number of his patients who had been abused by their own natural fathers that he felt forced to explain it away as fantasy; today we have begun to admit it is a truth so horrible that we have always been afraid to recognize it.

13. Feminists' earlier recognized that in a substantial number of cases of child battering and even some sexual abuse, the mother is the abuser, but this knowledge has mysteriously been buried under false charges about a presumed male monopoly on violence and tabloid-style scandal about 'rings' of child abusers.

14. For example, see: Knupfer, Genevieve; Clark, Walter and Room, Robin, 'The Mental Health of the Unmarried', *The American Journal of Psychiatry*, 122, February 1966; and Jessie Bernard's *The Future of Marriage*, Bantam, New York, 1972.

15. None of this is helped by the fact that in our society, 'sex' is frequently defined as copulation, as if all the other things women like – cuddling, stroking, and generally getting turned on – are not 'sex', but rather 'foreplay', somewhere lower on the hierarchy of male–female interaction. Although both males and females do enjoy other kinds of sex, this creates an interesting tautology in which the sex women generally enjoy is simply redefined as 'not sex' and even the most thoroughly unenjoyable act of copulation is 'real sex', so that it is not surprising if women appear not to like 'sex'.

16. Hard-core pornography – all too often used by anti-porn campaigners to exemplify porngraphy that should be banned

in this country – is for the most part already illegal in the United Kingdom. The extreme language and lurid descriptions of 'violent, degrading porn' which are used to arouse outrage and generate support for further anti-porn legislation are completely inappropriate when applied to the kind of sexual material currently available here. (In truth, *most* pornography in Europe and the English-speaking world is far less violent than mainstream media.) Campaign Against Pornography speakers have been heard to justify the 'Off the Shelf' campaign by claiming you can find snuff films on the top shelf at W.H. Smith; in fact, no actual snuff film has ever been known to exist. (See 'Snuff: Believing the Worst', in this volume.) Indeed, pornographic videos are generally illegal, depiction of erect organs or penetration with objects has been deemed to be in violation of the Obscene Publications Acts, and the two major news chains – W.H. Smith and John Menzies – will not carry sexually oriented magazines that show people together. This makes it virtually impossible to show mutuality between people or to portray men sexually in the same way that women are portrayed; ironically, anti-porn campaigners criticize porn, rather than censorship, for creating this imbalance.

17. CPC distinguish between 'pornography', which they say degrades women, and 'erotica', which they say does not degrade women. Unlike Campaign Against Pornography, CPC speakers, when pressed, say they believe the Obscene Publications Acts should be eliminated and replaced with legislation similar to that which Dworkin and MacKinnon have proposed in the US. CPC is somewhat less likely than CAP to insist that all sexually explicit imagery is degrading to women, but it's hard to pin them down on what 'erotica' looks like.

18. See *Hard Core*, by Linda Williams (Pandora Press, London, 1990) for a fascinating examination of pornographic film from a feminist perspective.

19. For the text of the Minneapolis hearings, see *Pornography and Sexual Violence: Evidence of the Links*, Everywoman Limited, London, 1988.

1 Misguided, Dangerous and Wrong

1. There is a discussion of the early roots of anti-pornography analysis in feminism in Echols, Alice, *Daring To Be Bad:*

Radical Feminism in America 1967–1975, University of Minnesota Press, Minneapolis, 1989, pp. 288–91, 360–64n.

2. Lederer, Laura, *Take Back the Night: Women on Pornography*, William Morrow, New York, 1980, pp. 15–16, 23.

3. Emblematic anthologies from this period of feminism include such classics as Gornick, Vivien and Moran, Barbara K., *Women in Sexist Society: Studies in Power and Powerlessness*, Basic Books, New York, 1971; Baker Miller, Jean, *Psychoanalysis and Women*, Penguin, Baltimore, 1973; Mitchell, Juliet and Oakley, Ann, *The Rights and Wrongs of Women*, Harmondsworth, Middlesex, England, 1976; Koedt, Anne; Levine, Ellen; Rapone, Anita, *Radical Feminism*, Quadrangle, New York, 1973; Morgan, Robin, *Sisterhood is Powerful*, Vintage, New York, 1970.

4. For example, see Russell, Diana E.H. and Lederer, Laura, 'Questions We Are Asked Most Often', in Lederer, 1980, op. cit., pp. 23–9.

5. I have attended many educational presentations by WAVPM and WAP, and in none of them was any questioning of their basic assumptions permitted. Questions were restricted to inquiries about implementing their programme, and those who tried to raise other issues were ignored or dismissed. For similar experiences, see two accounts of WAP's slide show and tour in Webster, Paula, 'Pornography and Pleasure', *Sex Issue, Heresies*, 12, 1981, pp. 48–51 and D'Emilio, John, 'Women Against Pornography', *Christopher Street*, May 1980, pp. 19–26.

6. The rhetorical attacks have heated up in the interim. Now feminists who reject anti-porn dogma are called 'Uncle Toms,' accused of supporting male supremacy, and described as attacking feminism.

   In this regard exemplary texts are Jeffreys, Sheila, *Anticlimax: A Feminist Perspective on the Sexual Revolution*, The Women's Press, London, 1990, pp. 260–86; and Leidholdt, Dorchen and Raymond, Janice G., *The Sexual Liberals and the Attack on Feminism*, Pergamon, New York, 1990. In *Pornography and Civil Rights: A New Day For Women's Equality*, Organizing Against Pornography, Minneapolis, 1988, Catharine MacKinnon and Andrea Dworkin state 'There is no viable propornography feminism. Our legitimate differences centre on *how* to fight pornography' [p.83, their emphasis].

   See also MacKinnon, Catharine A., *Feminism Unmodified: Discourses on Life and Law*, Cambridge, Massachusetts, 1987, p. 146: 'A critique of pornography is to feminism what its defence is to male supremacy.' I disagree. In MacKinnon's work and that of other anti-porn feminists, the critique of pornography has been substituted for a critique of male supremacy.

7. Such terminological confusions continue to bedevil feminist discourse. The more updated version is to use pornography as a synonym for the subordination of women itself, and to equate opposition to pornography with opposition to male supremacy.

8. Willis, Ellen, *Beginning To See the Light*, Alfred Knopf, New York, 1981, pp. 145–46. As Willis wryly puts it, 'the feminist bias is that women are equal to men and the male chauvinist bias is that women are inferior. The unbiased view is that the truth lies somewhere in between.' I often rephrase her comment as follows: the view of gay activism is that homosexuals deserve equality and respect. The view of neo-fascist homophobes is that homosexuals are diseased and should be incarcerated, punished, or exterminated. What, pray tell, is the position in the middle?

9. In addition to the Lederer collection, other major anti-porn texts include Dworkin, Andrea, *Pornography: Men Possessing Women*, Perigee, New York, 1981; Dworkin, Andrea, *Right-Wing Women*, Perigee, New York, 1983; Griffin, Susan, *Pornography and Silence: Culture's Revenge Against Nature*, Harper Colophon, New York, 1981; Dworkin, Andrea and MacKinnon, Catharine A., *Pornography and Civil Rights: A New Day for Women's Equality*, Organizing Against Pornography, Minneapolis, 1988; MacKinnon, Catharine A., *Toward a Feminist Theory of the State*, Harvard University Press, Cambridge, Massachusetts, 1989; MacKinnon, Catharine A., *Feminism Unmodified: Discourses on Life and Law*, Harvard University Press, Cambridge, Massachusetts, 1987; Brownmiller, Susan, *Against Our Will: Men, Women, and Rape*, Bantam, New York, 1976; Barry, Kathleen, *Female Sexual Slavery*, Prentice-Hall, Englewood Cliffs, New Jersey, 1979.

10. San Francisco's *On Our Backs*, Boston's *Bad Attitude* and *Outrageous Women*, Britain's *Quim* and Australia's *Wicked Women* are a few of these lesbian oriented sexual publications. All have encountered governmental or community censorship.

11. Russell and Lederer, op. cit., p. 24. The Kearny and the North Beach were the two theatres that catered to the bondage crowd. When asked 'what kinds of images are you talking

about when you say you are opposed to "violence in pornography and media"?'the response was,'We are talking about films like the ones shown in the Kearny Cinema in San Francisco'.

12. Dworkin is referring to this spread when she complains that '*Penthouse* hangs Asian women from trees'. Dworkin, Andrea and MacKinnon, Catherine A., *Pornography and Civil Rights: A New Day for Women's Equality*, p. 63.

13. There was a movement in the early 1980s to produce commercial SM erotica made by and for SM practitioners, which resulted in successful and now classic films such as *Story of K.*, The Film Company, 1980, and *Journey Into Pain*, Loving SM Productions, 1983. Ironically, none of these films are currently available due to the increasingly harsh legal climate for sexual materials in the United States.

14. For the slide shows, see Webster, op. cit., and D'Emilio, op. cit. *Not A Love Story: A Film About Pornography* purports to be a documentary of pornography. It was directed by Bonnie Sherr Klein and produced by Dorothy Todd Henaut, Studio D., National Film Board of Canada, 1981.

15. See for instance 'The Psychology of Homosexuality', ISIS, Lincoln, Nebraska, 1984; 'AIDS, the Blood Supply, and Homosexuality (What Homosexuals Do In Public Is Offensive, What they Do in Private is Deadly', ISIS, Lincoln, Nebraska, 1985; 'What Homosexuals Do (Its More than Merely Disgusting)', ISIS, Lincoln, Nebraska, 1985; 'Criminality, Social Disruption, and Homosexuality (Homosexuality is a Crime against Humanity)', ISIS, Lincoln, Nebraska, 1985; 'Homosexuality and the AIDS threat to the Nation's Blood Supply', ISIS, Lincoln, Nebraska, 1985; 'Child Molestation and Homosexuality (Homosexuality is a Crime against Humanity)', ISIS, Lincoln, Nebraska, 1985.

16. 'Murder, Violence, and Homosexuality (What Homosexuals Do in Public is Offensive, What they Do in Private is Deadly!)', ISIS, Lincoln, Nebraska, 1985. In the same pamphlet, Cameron claims that the Nazis 'started out as a gay rights party'.

17. Kendrick, Walter, *The Secret Museum: Pornography in Modern Culture*, Viking, New York, 1987.

18. As I prepare this manuscript for publication, there is proposed Federal legislation along these lines. See note 42, below.

19. Longino, Helen E., 'Pornography, Oppression, and Freedom: A Closer Look', Lederer, op. cit., pp. 40–54, especially 42–46.

20. Dworkin, Andrea and MacKinnon, Catharine A., *Pornography and Civil Rights*, op. cit., p. 36. See also MacKinnon, *Feminism Unmodified*, op. cit., p. 148.
21. Hearings on Pornography, National Organization for Women, San Francisco, CA, 26 March 1986.
22. Attorney General's Commission on Pornography, *Final Report*, US Department of Justice, July 1986; Vance, Carole, 'Negotiating Sex and Gender in the Attorney General's Commission on Pornography' in Faye Ginsburg and Anna L. Tsing, *Uncertain Terms: Negotiating Gender in American Culture*, Beacon Press, Boston, 1990, or in Lynne Segal and Mary McIntosh, *Sex Exposed: Sexuality and the Pornography Debate*, Virago, London, 1992. Some states have now banned dildos and artificial vaginas, and in a 1985 decision the Supreme Court of Canada ruled that penis-shaped vibrators and inflatable dolls were 'obscene'.
23. Willis, Ellen, untitled columns, *Village Voice*, 15 October 1979, p. 8, and 12 November 1979, p. 8. These two splendid pieces were reprinted as 'Feminism, Moralism, and Pornography', in *Beginning to See the Light: Pieces of a Decade*, op. cit.
24. Steinem, Gloria, 'Erotica and Pornography: A Clear and Present Danger', *Ms*, November, 1978, pp. 53–4, 75, 78.
25. Dworkin, *Pornography*, op. cit., preface. Indeed, she could not have said it better: 'erotica is simply high-class pornography: better produced, better conceived, better executed, better packaged, designed for a better class of consumer'.
26. Stein, Rob, 'Medical School Sex Film Wars,' *San Francisco Examiner*, 15 January 1986, pp. AA–55.
27. McCormack, Thelma, 'Appendix I: Making Sense of the Research on Pornography', in Varda Burstyn, *Women Against Censorship*, Douglas and McIntyre, Vancouver, 1985; and Henry, Alice, 'Porn Is Subordination?', *Off Our Backs*, November 1984, pp. 20, 24. Prior to this article, Alice Henry had often expressed support of anti-porn politics in the pages of *Off Our Backs*, but in this incisive essay even she expressed scepticism of the claims about empirical research (as well as the wisdom of new anti-porn legislation). [Editors' note: See also King, Alison, 'Mystery & Imagination: The Case of Pornography Effects Studies', this volume.]
28. Donnerstein, Edward, 'Aggressive Erotica and Violence Against Women', *Journal of Personality and Social Psychology*, 1990,

vol. 39, no. 2, pp. 269–77; and Malamuth Neal M., and Donnerstein, Edward, *Pornography and Sexual Aggression*, Academic Press, New York, 1984.

29. Zillman, Dolf and Bryant, Jennings, 'Effects of Massive Exposure to Pornography', in Malamuth and Donnerstein, op. cit., pp. 115–38; 'X-Rated Flicks Cool People to Real-Life Sex', *San Francisco Examiner*, 23 April 1986, p. A7.

30. Donnerstein, Edward I. and Linz, Daniel G., 'The Question of Pornography: It is not Sex, but Violence, that is an Obscenity in Our Society', *Psychology Today*, December 1986, pp. 56–9; Goldman, Daniel, 'Researchers Dispute Pornography Report on Link to Violence', *New York Times*, 17 May 1986, pp. 1, 7; Donnerstein, Dr Edward, 'Interview,' *Penthouse*, September 1985, pp. 165–68,180–81.

 This entire section is the most out of date, and would have required complete revision to fix. I elected to leave it alone; however, there has been a deluge of material on this point in the years since the piece was written. Most germane is Edward Donnerstein, Daniel Linz, and Steven Penrod, *The Question of Pornography: Research Findings and Policy Implications*, The Free Press, New York, 1987, particularly Chapter 6, 'Is it the Sex or Is it the Violence?' The book also contains a critique of the misuse of the research data by the Meese Commission. Two of the female members of the Meese Commission, Dr Judith Becker and Ellen Levine, included harsh criticisms of the conclusions of the Commission and the process by which these conclusions were reached. In their dissenting report, they noted that 'it is essential to state that the social science research has not been designed to evaluate the relationship between exposure to pornography and the commission of sexual crimes; therefore efforts to tease the current data into proof of a causal link between these acts simply cannot be accepted. Furthermore, social science does not speak to harm, on which this Commission report focuses.' (*Final Report*, op. cit., p. 204).

31. For a completely different perspective from that of the anti-pornography movement on the relationship between violence and women's subordination, see Baron, Larry, 'Pornography and Gender Equality: An Empirical Analysis', *Journal of Sex Research*, vol. 27, no. 3, August 1990, pp. 363–80.

32. Hearings on Pornography, op. cit.

33. Dworkin, *Pornography*, op. cit., p. 201.

34. Samois, *Coming To Power*, Alyson, Boston, 1987; Weinberg, Thomas and Kamel, G. W. Levi, *S and M: Studies in Sadomasochism*, Prometheus, Buffalo, 1983; Mains, Geoff, *Urban Aboriginals*, Gay Sunshine, San Francisco, 1984; Stoller, Robert, *Pain and Passion: A Psychoanalyst Explores the World of S&M*, Plenum, New York, 1991; Thompson, Mark, *Leatherfolk: Radical Sex, People, Politics, and Practice*, Alyson, Boston, 1991; Grumley, Michael and Gallucci, Ed, *Hard Corps: Studies in Leather and Sadomasochism*, Dutton, New York, 1977; Rosen, Michael, *Sexual Magic: The S/M Photographs*, Shaynew Press, San Francisco, 1986; and Rosen, Michael, *Sexual Portraits: Photographs of Radical Sexuality*, Shaynew Press, San Francisco, 1990.

35. Hearings on Pornography, op. cit.

36. Delacoste, Frederique and Alexander, Priscilla, *Sex Work: Writings by Women in the Sex Industry*, Cleis Press, San Francisco, 1987; Jaget, Claude, *Prostitutes: Our Life*, Falling Wall Press, Bristol, 1980; Pheterson, Gail, *A Vindication of the Rights of Whores*, Seal Press, Seattle, 1989; James, Jennifer, et al., *The Politics of Prostitution*, Social Research Associates, Seattle, 1977.

37. Dworkin, *Pornography*, op. cit., p. 200, my emphasis.

38. Dworkin, *Right Wing Women*, op. cit., p. 223, my emphasis.

39. Dworkin, ibid., pp. 222, 228, 229.

40. Dworkin, *Pornography*, op. cit., pp. 199–200. This dubious history and phony etymology appears repeatedly throughout the anti-porn literature where it is often used as a key argument against pornography. In *Pornography and Civil Rights*, op. cit., p. 74, MacKinnon and Dworkin state that 'We can trace pornography without any difficulty back as far as ancient Greece in the west. Pornography is a Greek word ... It refers to writing, etching, or drawing of women who, in real life, were kept in female sexual slavery in ancient Greece. Pornography has always, as far back as we can go, had to do with exploiting, debasing, and violating women in forced sex.' In the *Ms* article cited above, Gloria Steinem employs it as the basis of her erotica/pornography distinction.

41. Actually, as Kendrick points out (op. cit., p. 11) the term did exist in ancient Greece. But it appears so rarely in the surviving Greek texts that it could not have been indicative of a significant category of ancient experience, let alone one that so closely approximates the opinions of sexual materials held by Dworkin or nineteenth-century scholars (John J. Winkler, personal communication, 1986).

42. This has indeed been the case. When I submitted the earlier version of this essay in 1986, I enclosed California Assembly

Bill No. 3645, in which the diffusion of anti-porn ideas into legal initiatives was already apparent. AB 3645 did not pass. But as this essay goes to press, Senate Bill 1521, the Pornography Victims Compensation Act, is poised to become federal law. It makes pornography a cause of civil action, as was proposed in the MacKinnon/Dworkin ordinance, and allows 'victims' to sue not their perpetrators but the makers and distributors of any obscene material that may have influenced their perpetrators. In contrast to the original MacKinnon/Dworkin approach, this bill is based on a traditional legal definition of obscenity rather than the so-called 'feminist' definition in the Indianapolis ordinance.

If this bill becomes law, when some lunatic who has read porn or seen a pornographic film decides to go on a rampage, the producers and distributors of his reading material may be held accountable for his behaviour and sued in federal court. The bill establishes third-party liability, but only for the producers and distributors of sexual media. The same kind of liability has been ruled unconstitutional in the case of non-obscene media. But since obscenity is not constitutionally protected speech, SB 1521 may be upheld in the courts.

And what will happen if the same lunatic, after reading his Bible, goes out and murders a bunch of prostitutes (not an altogether unusual occurrence)? The churches and religious publishers will not be held accountable when murderers claim biblical authority.

43. This has also come to pass. The Meese Commission released its *Final Report* in July of 1986. The report included a long wish list of new obscenity legislation and suggested procedures to increase enforcement of existing law at the local, state and federal levels. Much of the anti-porn agenda articulated in the report has become law, policy and common practice. The US Department of Justice duly created an obscenity enforcement unit, increased obscenity prosecutions, began to bring forfeiture proceedings against those convicted of obscenity offences, and started a national computerized data bank on producers, distributors and consumers of sexually explicit material (ACLU Arts Censorship Project, *Above the Law: The Justice Department's War Against the First Amendment*, American Civil Liberties Union, Medford, New York, 1991).

The obscenity unit was recently renamed the 'Child Exploitation and Obscenity Unit'. The irony of this new title is that there has been no commercial child pornography available in the United States since the late 1970s. In its efforts to entrap suspected paedophiles, the federal government has become the largest (and only) distributor of child pornography in the United States. For a longer discussion of the right-wing war on porn and of the collaboration of anti-porn feminists, see my afterword to a reprint of 'Thinking Sex: Notes for a Radical Theory of the Politics of Sexuality', in Kauffman, Linda S., *American Feminist Thought, 1982–1992*, Basil Blackwell, Oxford, forthcoming.

4 Changing Perceptions in the Feminist Debate

1. The word 'working' here is used in deference to the popular assumption that only people who have interesting or high-status jobs are 'professionals', but of course all jobs done for money are 'professional' work, and these are the kinds of job we are referring to. Many women work very hard in jobs that don't pay – such as housewives – and we are not happy with a convention that perceives such women as 'not working' merely because they are not being paid.

2. Perhaps this is most obvious in the way that women are desexualized at precisely the age at which they are considered to be worthless as mothers and nurturers, despite the fact there is no evidence whatsoever that women are less sexual at that age.

3. This is the underlying assumption in defence arguments in rape trials. The very idea that men are 'provoked' to rape women who wear miniskirts or allow themselves to be alone with men suggests that males are out of control to begin with and that it is the obligation of women not to stir them to sexual thoughts. This is why even women who have been beaten bloody by their assailants can be accused of 'asking for' rape – their failure to supress all possibility of sexual thoughts is, in effect, a social crime deserving brutal punishment.

5 Mystery and Imagination

Abel, G.G. et al., 'The Components of Rapists' Sexual Arousal', *Archives of General Psychiatry*, 34, 1977.

Abel, G.G. et al., 'Differentiating Sexual Aggressiveness With Penile Measures', *Criminal Justice and Behavior*, 5, 1978.

Abel, G.G. et al., 'Measurement of Sexual Arousal in Several Para-philiacs: The Effect of Stimulus Modality, Instructional Set and

Stimulus Content on the Objectives', *Behavioral Research & Therapy*, 19, 1981.

Abel, G.G. et al., 'The Effects of Erotica on Paraphiliacs' Behavior', unpub. man., 1985.

Amendolia, M. and Thompson W., 'Survey on Sexual Attitudes Concerning Data and Acquaintance Rape', unpub. pilot study, Reading University, 1991.

Baron, R.A., 'Sexual Arousal and Physical Aggression: The Inhibiting Influence of "Cheese Cake" and Nudes', *Bulletin of Psychonomic Society*, 3, 1974a.

Baron, R.A., 'The Aggression-Inhibiting Influence of Heightened Sexual Arousal', *Journal of Personality and Social Psychology*, 30, 3, 1974b.

Baron, R.A., *Human Aggression*, Plenium, New York, 1977.

Baron, R.A., 'Heightened Sexual Arousal and Physical Aggression: An Extension of Females', *Journal of Research in Personality*, 13, 1979.

Baron, R.A. and Bell, P.A., 'Effects of Heightened Sexual Arousal on Physical Aggression', American Psychological Association, Proceedings, 8, 1973.

Baron, R.A. and Bell, P.A., 'Sexual Arousal and Aggression by Males: Effects of Type of Erotic Stimuli and Prior Provocation', *Journal of Personality and Social Psychology*, 35, 2, 1977.

Baron, L. and Straus, M.A., 'Sexual Stratification, Pornography, and Rape in the United States', N.M. Malamuth and E. Donnerstein (ed.) *Pornography and Sexual Aggression*, 1984.

Baron, L. and Straus, M.A., 'Legitimate Violence, Pornography, and Sexual Inequality as Explanations for State and Regional Differences in Rape', unpub. man., 1985.

Baron, L. and Straus, M.A., 'Rape and its Relation to Social Disorganization, Pornography, and Sexual Inequality in the United States', unpub. man., 1986.

Baxter, D.J. et al., 'Sexual Responses to Consenting And Forced Sex in a Large Sample of Rapists', *Behavioural Research & Therapy*, 24, 1986.

Berkowitz, L. and Donnerstein, E., 'External Validity is more than Skin Deep', *American Psychologist*, 37, 1982.

Burt, M.E.H., 'Use of Pornography by Women; A Critical review of the Literature', *Case Western Reserve Journal of Sociology*, 8, 1976.

Cantor, J. et al., 'Female Responses to Provocation After Exposure to Aggressive and Erotic Films', *Communication Research*, 5, 1978.

Cash, T.F. et al., '"Mirror, mirror, on the Wall …?": Contrasts Effects and Self-evaluations of Physical Attractiveness', *Personality and Social Psychology Bulletin*, 9, 1983.

Check, J.V.P., 'The Hostility Toward Women Scale', unpub. Diss., 1985.

Cook, R.F. et al., 'Pornography and the Sex Offender: Patterns of Previous Exposure and Arousal Effects of Pornographic Stimuli', *Journal of Applied Psychology*, 55, 1987.

Court, J.H., 'Pornography and Sex-Crimes: a Re-evaluation in the Light of Recent Trends around the World', *International Journal of Criminology and Penology*, 5, 1976.

Court, J.H., 'Rape & Pornography in White South Africa', *Dejure*, 12, 1979.

Court, J.H., *Pornography: a Christian Critique*, Illinois, 1980a.

Court, J.H., *Pornography & the Harm Condition*, Adelaide, 1980b.

Court, J.H., 'Pornography: an Update', *British Journal of Sexual Medicine*, May 1981.

Court, J.H., 'Rape and Trends in New South Wales: a Discussion of Conflicting Evidence', *Australian Journal of Social Issues* , 17, 1982.

Dietz, P.E. et al., 'Detective Magazines: Pornography for the Sexual Sadist?', *Journal of Forensic Sciences*, 31(1), 1986.

Donnerstein, E., 'Pornography: its Effect on Violence Against Women', N. Malamuth and E. Donnerstein (eds.) *Pornography and Sexual Aggression*, 1984.

Donnerstein, E. and Barrett, G., 'The Effects of Erotic Stimuli on Male Aggression Towards Females', *Journal of Personality and Social Psychology*, 36, 1978.

Donnerstein, E. and Berkowitz, L., 'Victim Reactions in Aggressive Erotic Films as a Factor in Violence Against Women', *Journal of Personality and Social Psychology*, 41, 1981.

Donnerstein, E. and Hallam, J., 'Facilitating Effects of Erotica on Aggression Against Women', *Journal of Personality and Social Psychology*, 36, 1978.

Donnerstein, E. et al., 'Erotic Stimuli and Aggression: Facilitation or Inhibition?', *Journal of Personality and Social Psychology*, 32, 1975.

Donnerstein, E. et al., 'Role of Aggressive and Sexual Images in Violent Pornography', unpub. man., reported in Donnerstein et al., *The Question of Pornography*, 1986.

Donnerstein, E. et al., *The Question of Pornography*, New York, 1987.

Fisher, W.A. and Grenier G., 'Failures to Replicate Effects of Pornography on Attitudes and Behavior: the Emperor Has No Clothes', unpub. man., 1988.

Fisher, J.L. and Harris, M.B., 'Modelling, Arousal and Aggression', *Journal of Social Psychology*, 100, 1976.

Frodi, A., 'Sexual Arousal, Situational Restrictiveness and Aggressive Behaviour', *Journal Of Research In Personality*, 11, 1977.

Goldstein, M.J. et al., 'Pornography and Sexual Deviance: a Report of the Legal and Behavioral Institute', 1973.

Groth, N.A. and Hobson, W.F., 'The Dynamics of Sexual Assault', L.B. Schlesinger and E. Revitch (eds.), *Sexual Dynamics of Anti-Social Behavior*, 1983.

Jaffe, Y. et al., 'Sexual Arousal and Behavioural Aggression', *Journal of Personality and Social Psychology*, 30, 1974.

Kant, H.S. and Goldstein, M.J., 'Pornography and its Effects, in D. Savitz and J. Johnson (eds.), *Crime in Society*, 1978.

Kelley, K., 'Sexual Attitudes as Determinants of the Motivational Properties of Exposure to Erotica', *Personality and Individual Differences*, 6, 1985.

Kelley, K., 'Prosocial Responding and Affect Induction: Sex Differences Following Exposure to Sexually Explicit Slides', quoted in Kelley, K. et al., 'Three Faces of Sexual Explicitness', in D. Zillmann and J. Bryant (eds.), *Pornography: Research Advances and Policy Considerations*, 1989.

Kelley, K. and Musialowski, D., 'Female Sexual Victimization and Effects of Warnings about Violent Pornography', paper presented at the Eastern Psychological Association, New York, 1986.

Krafka, C.L., 'Sexually Explicit, Sexually Violent, and Violent Media: Effects of Multiple Naturalistic Exposures and Debriefing on Female Viewers', unpub. doc. diss., Wisconsin, 1985.

Langevin, R. et al., 'Are Rapists Sexually Anomalous, Aggressive, or Both?', in R. Langevin (ed.), *Erotic Preference, Gender Identity, and Aggression in Men: New Research Studies*, 1985.

Leonard, K.E. and Taylor, S.P., 'Exposure to Pornography, Permissive and Non-permissive Cues, and Male Aggression toward Females', *Motivation and Emotion*, 7, 1983.

Linz, D., 'Sexual Violence in the Media: Effects on Male Viewers and Implications for Society', unpub. doc. diss., 1985.

Linz, D. et al., 'The Effects of Multiple Exposures to Filmed Violence Against Women', *Journal of Communication*, 34, 1984.

Malamuth, N., 'Aggression Against Women: Cultural and Individual Causes', in N. Malamuth and E. Donnerstein (eds.), *Pornography and Sexual Aggression*, Academic Press, 1984.

Malamuth, N., 'Erotica, Aggression and Perceived Appropriateness', paper presented at the AM of the American Psychological Association, 1978.

Malamuth, N. and Ceniti, J., 'Repeated Exposure to Violent and Non-Violent Pornography: Likelihood of Raping Ratings and Laboratory Aggression Against Women', *Aggressive Behavior*, 12, 1986.

Malamuth, N. and Check, J.V.P., 'Penile Tumescence and Perceptual Responses to Rape as a Function of Victim's Perceived Reactions', *Journal of Applied Social Psychology*, 10, 1980.

Malamuth, N. and Check, J.V.P., 'The Effects of Aggressive Pornography on beliefs of Rape Myths: Individual Differences', *Journal of Research in Personality*, 19, 1985.

Malamuth, N.M. and Donnerstein, E., *Pornography and Sexual Aggression*, Academic Press, 1984.

Malamuth, N. et al., 'Testing Hypothesis Regarding Rape: Exposure to Sexual Violence, Sex Differences and the "Normality" of Rapists', *Journal of Research in Personality*, 14, 1980.

Malamuth, N. et al., 'Sexual Arousal in Response to Aggression: Ideological, Aggressive, and Sexual Correlates', *Journal Of Personality & Social Psychology*, 50, 1986.

Marshall, W.L., 'Pornography and Sex Offenders', in Zillmann and Bryant, *Pornography: Research Advances and Policy Considerations*, 1989.

Marshall, W.L. et al., 'Sexual Offenders Against Female Children: Sexual Preference for Age, Victims and Type of Behaviour', *Canadian Journal of Behavioural Science*, 18, 1986.

McQuail, D., *Mass Communication Theory*, London, 1987.

Meese, E., *Attorney General's Commission on Pornography: Final Report*, vols. 1 and 2, Justice Dept., Washington, 1986.

Milgram, S., 'Behavioral Study of Obedience, *Journal Of Abnormal And Social Psychology*, 67, 1963.

Mosher, D.L., 'Sex Callousness Toward Women', *Technical Report of the Commission on Obscenity and Pornography*, vol. 7, 1970.

Mueller, C.W. and Donnerstein, E., 'Film-Facilitated Arousal and Prosocial Behaviour', *Journal of Experimental Social Psychology*, 17, 1981.

Osanka, F.M. and Johann, S.E., *Sourcebook on Pornography*, Lexington, 1989.

Palys, T.S., 'Testing the Common Wisdom: the Social Content of Pornography', *Canadian Psychology*, 27(1), 1986.

Przybyla, D.P., 'The Facilitating Effects of Exposure to Erotica on Male Pro-social Behaviour', unpub. doc. diss., SUNY at Albany, 1985.

Quinsey, V.L. and Chaplin, T.C., 'Stimulus Control of Rapists and Non-Sex Offenders' Sexual Arousal', *Behavioral Assessment*, 6, 1984.

Rada, R.T., *Clinical Aspects of The Rapist*, New York, 1978.

Scott, J.E., 'Violence and Erotic Material: the Relationship between Adult Entertainment and Rape', paper presented at GM of the American Association for the Advancement of Science, Los Angeles, 1985.

Thompson, W., 'Porn-Wars', unpublished PhD thesis, Essex University, 1987.

Thompson, W. and Annetts, J., *Soft-Core*, GJW, 1990.

Thompson, W. et al., 'Legends, Panics, and Political Crusades: Snuff, Kiddie Cults, AIDS, and Other Horror Stories', paper presented to International Conference on Urban Legends, Sheffield, 1990.

Tong, R., *Feminist Thought*, Westview, 1989.

Walker, C.E., 'Erotic Stimuli and the Aggressive Sexual Offender', *Technical Reports of the Commission on Obscenity and Pornography*, vol. 7, 1970.

Weaver, J.B., 'Effects of Portrayals of Female Sexuality and Violence against Women on Percentages of Women', unpub. doc. diss., 1987.

White, L.A., 'Erotica and Aggression: the Influence of Sexual Arousal, Positive Effects and Negative Effects on Aggressive Behavior', *Journal of Personality And Social Psychology*, 34, 1979.

Wydra, A. et al., 'Identification of Cues and Control of Sexual Arousal by Rapists', *Behavioral Research and Therapy*, 21, 1983.

Zillmann, D., 'Excitation Transfer in Communication-Mediated Aggressive Behavior', *Journal of Experimental Social Psychology*, 7, 1971.

Zillmann, D., 'Effects of Prolonged Consumption of Pornography', D. Zillmann and J. Bryant (eds.), *Pornography: Research Advances and Policy Considerations*, 1989.

Zillmann, D. and Bryant, J., testimony presented to Meese Commission, 1985.

Zillmann, D. and Bryant, J., 'Pornography, Sexual Callousness and the Trivialization of Rape, *Journal of Communication*, 32, 1982.

Zillmann, D. and Bryant, J., 'Effects of Massive Exposure to Pornography', in N. Malamuth and E. Donnerstein (eds.) *Pornography and Sexual Aggression*, 1984.

Zillmann, D. and Bryant, J., 'Shifting Preferences in Pornography Consumption', *Communication Research*, 13, 1986.

Zillmann, D. and Bryant, J., 'Pornography's Impact on Sexual Satisfaction', *Journal of Applied Social Psychology*, 18, 1988.

Zillmann, D. and Bryant, J., *Pornography: Research Advances & Policy Considerations*, London, 1989.

Zillmann, D. and Sapolsky, B., 'What Mediates the Effect of Mild Erotica on Annoyance and Hostile Behavior in Males?', *Journal Of Personality And Social Psychology*, 35, 1977.

Zillmann, D. and Weaver, J.B., 'Pornography and Men's Sexual Callousness towards Women', in D. Zillmann and J. Bryant (eds.), *Pornography: Research Advances and Policy Considerations*, 1989.

Zillmann, D. et al., 'Excitation and Hedonic Valance in the Effect of Erotica on Motivated Intermale Aggression', *European Journal of Social Psychology*, 11, 1981.

6 Essentially Sex

1. See, for example, Braidotti, Rosi, *Patterns of Dissonance, a Study of Women in Contemporary Philosophy*, Polity Press, Cambridge, 1991; Spivak, Gyatri, 'Subaltern Studies: Deconstructing Historiography', in *In Other Words: Essays in Cultural Politics*, Methuen, London and New York, 1987; and Fuss, Diana, *Essentially Speaking*, Routledge, London, 1989.

2. See, for example, Plummer, K., 'Sexual Diversity: A Sociological Perspective', in K. Howells (ed.), *The Psychology of Sexual Diversity*, Blackwell, Oxford, 1984, pp. 219–53.

3. Reich, W., *The Function of the Orgasm*, trans. T.P. Wolfe, New York, 1961, p. 79.

4. Freud, S., *The Three Essays on Sexuality*, Penguin, London, 1977.

5. Freud, S., Standard Edition, vol. VII, ed. Strachey, Hogarth, London, 1953–1974, p.135.

6. See, for example, L'Esperance, J., 'Doctors and Women in the 19th Century: Sexuality and Role', in *Health Care & Popular Medicine in 19th Century England*, J. Woodward and D. Richards, (eds.), Croom Helm, London, 1977.

7. Weeks, J., *Sexuality.*, Routledge, London, 1986, p. 296.
8. Ibid., p. 299.
9. Wittig, Monique, 'The Category of Sex', *Feminist Issues*, 1982, p. 63–9.
10. Butler, J., 'Gender Trouble', *Feminism and the Subversion of Identity*, Routledge, London, 1990.
11. Jeffreys, Sheila, *Anticlimax*, The Women's Press, London, 1989.
12. Weeks, J., op. cit., p. 15.
13. Ibid. p. 27.
14. Foucault, Michel, *The History of Sexuality*, vol. 1, 'An Introduction', Robert Hurley, Allen Lane, New York, 1979, p. 28.
15. Ibid., p. 116.
16. See Jacques Lacan, *Ecrits*, trans. Alan Sheridan, W.W. Norton & Co., New York, 1977.
17. Weeks, J., 'Questions of Identity', in Pat Kaplan (ed.), *The Cultural Construction of Sexuality*, Tavistock Publications, London, 1987, p. 32.
18. Ibid p.33.
19. See ibid., p. 43.
20. Rich, Adrienne, 'Compulsory Heterosexuality and Lesbian Existence', in Ann Snitow, Christine Stansell and Sharon Thompson (eds.), *Desire: The Politics of Sexuality*, Virago, London, 1984.
21. Plummer, K., 'Sexual Diversity: A Sociological Perspective', in K. Howells (ed.), *The Psychology of Sexual Diversity*, Blackwell, Oxford, 1984, pp. 219–53.
22. Hastrup, K., 'The Semantics of Biology: Virginity', in S. Ardener (ed.), *Defining Females: The Nature of Women in Society*, John Wiley, New York, 1978, pp. 49–65.
23. Rorty, Richard, quoted in O'Farrell, C., *Foucault: Historian or Philosopher*, Macmillan, London, 1989.
24. Fraser, Nancy, *Unruly Practices: Power, Discourse & Gender in Contemporary Social Theory*, Polity Press, Cambridge, 1989, p. 62.
25. Plato, *Symposium*, trans. W. Hamilton, Penguin, Harmondsworth, 1980.
26. Aristotle, *Ethics*, Penguin, Harmondsworth, 1980, p. 229.
27. See, for example, Kerr, Fergus, 'Charity as Friendship', in Brian Davies (ed.), *Language, Meaning and God; Essays in Honour of Herbert McCabe*, Geoffrey Chapman, London, 1987.
28. Bataille, G., *Eroticism*, Marian Boyars, London and New York, 1987, p. 167.

29. Plato, op. cit.
30. Goodison, Lucy, 'Really Being in Love Means Wanting to Live in a Different World', in J. Ryan and S. Cartledge (eds.), *Sex and Love, New Thoughts on Old Contradictions*, The Women's Press, London, 1983.
31. Braidotti, Rosi, *Patterns of Disonance: A Study of Women in Contemporary Philosophy*, Polity Press, Cambridge, 1991.
32. Foucault, M. and Sennett, R., 'Sexuality & Solitude' in *Constructing Sexuality*, Junction Books, London, 1981, p. 175.
33. Ibid., p. 176.
34. Ibid., p. 176.

7 The Small Matter of Children

1. Owens, Tuppy, *The Betrayal of Youth: Radical Perspectives of Childhood Sexuality, Intergenerational Sex and the Sexual Oppression of Children and Young People*, Warren Middleton (ed.), CL Publications, 1986.
2. Nestle, Joan, *A Restricted Country*, Sheba Press, 1987.
3. Rubin, Gayle, 'Thinking Sex: Notes for a Radical Theory of the Politics of Sexuality', in Carole S. Vance (ed.), *Pleasure & Danger: Exploring Female Sexuality*, Routledge and Keegan Paul, 1984.
4. 'The Witch-Hunt Must Stop', NAMBLA Bulletin, March 1992.
5. See Langfield, T., 'Aspects of Sexual Development: Problems and Therapy in Children', in *Proceedings of the International Symposium on Childhood and Sexuality*, Edudes Vivantees, J.M. Samson, Montreal, 1980; Masters and Johnson, *Human Sexual Response*, Little Brown, Boston, 1966; *The Kinsey Institute New Report on Sex – What you must know to be Sexually Literate*, June M. Reinisch, PhD. with Ruth Beasley, MLS, St. Martin's Press, New York, 1990 and Penguin, London, 1991.
6. Ford, Nicholas, *Socio-Sexual Lifestyles of Young People in Southwest England*, Southwestern Regional Health Authority, 1991.
7. It is astonishing, in fact, that this is often just where women's denial of child sexuality stops – they perceive children as sexless right up until they realize that their daughters have been victimized by their own husbands or even by the milkman, at which point their 'innocent baby' becomes transformed into a seductive nymphette.
8. In Holland there have been helplines where children can call up to discuss assaults or difficulties in sexual relationships in

complete confidence. This gives children the opportunity to discuss experiences privately without the fear of the whole world coming down on their heads. In Britain, any query a child might make to a social worker immediately involves, by law, putting the entire legal circus into operation.

9 Snuff

1. Although some people, particularly in the feminist movement, have tried to re-define 'pornography' to mean something which is necessarily sexist, violent and indefensible, I use the definition of pornography that is understood by those who make it, those who buy it, and most anti-censorship and traditional anti-pornography campaigners: sexually explicit material intended to arouse sexually. Most people know that when they are talking about pornography, they are talking not about depictions of violence but about depictions of sex. Movies that concentrate on violence, like 'slasher movies', are a separate genre from pornography. Some of them certainly exploit sexual imagery from time to time, but that is not their principal subject matter.
2. The film makers were Roberta and Michael Findlay, who had shot the film as *Slaughterhouse* in 1971. Industry gossip is that Monarch Releasing Corporation's Alan Shackleton came up with the new ending and title.
3. Williams, Linda, *Hard Core*, Pandora Press, London, 1990.

10 Fear of Pornography

An earlier version of this piece was published as 'I'd Rather Be Drunk' in *I, Claudia*, a Class Whore Publication, available from Claudia, BM Claudia, London WC1N 3XX.

1. Millett, Kate, *Sexual Politics*, Avon Equinox Edition, 1971, p. 123.
2. Rogers, Barbara, 'Pornography and Sexual Violence', *Everywoman*, February 1988.
3. *Everywoman*, December 1990.
4. Schechter, Susan, *Women and Male Violence*, South End Press, 1971, p. 239.
5. Anti-pornography activist and author Andrea Dworkin shares a home with activist-author John Stoltenberg.

6. Hoagland, Sarah Lucia, 'Sadism, Masochism and Lesbian Feminism', in Robin Ruth Linden and others (ed.), *Against Sadomasochism*, Frog in the Well, 1982.
7. See, for example, Brownmiller, Susan, *Against Our Will: Men, Women and Rape*, Simon & Schuster, 1975.
8. Cartland, Barbara, *Book of Love and Lovers*, Michael Joseph, 1978, p. 151.

Conclusion

1. Millett, Kate, *Sexual Politics*, Avon Equinox Edition, 1971.
2. See 'Misguided, Dangerous, and Wrong' by Gayle Rubin, this volume.
3. Some people did, however, believe that women should not seek employment outside the home, and took the opportunity to say so. The International Ladies Garment Workers' Union expressed a different position. Nor is this all ancient history. In their review of 1991 events, *Ms.* magazine reports the deaths of 18 women and seven men when the poultry-processing plant in Hamlet, North Carolina, where they worked, caught fire. 'Who killed Peggy Jean Anderson?' is the question *Ms* asks. Its deduction: 'Suspect 1: the owner who bolted the doors to prevent chicken parts being pilfered. Suspects 2 and 3: the Reagan and Bush administrations, which spent the last decade ignoring federal safety regulations in the workplace.' ('The Good, the Bad, and the Absurd ... Across the Country') Note that *Ms.* did not report that poultry is a multi-billion dollar industry, nor did it use this information to call for the elimination of the poultry business, although precisely this reasoning is cited in the same issue as a reason to eliminate the sex industry. (*Ms.* vol II, no 4, January/February 1992.)
4. Many people mistakenly believe that fat has been proven to cause heart disease. The truth is that we have seen correlations of obesity with heart disease, but have never found any causal relationship between the two. Fat people tend to suffer a lot of stress caused by the way society treats them – including poverty, because many employers will not hire fat people – and these things in themselves correlate with heart disease, whether or not obesity is present. Moreover, fat people try to relieve this stress by going on diets, and diets themselves often place enormous stress on the heart. In other words, for all we know, fat itself does not cause ill-health, but the ill-health

could be the result of poverty, societally caused stress, and dieting. For an effective refutation of most commonly held beliefs about fat, see *Shadow on a Tightrope: Writings by Women on Fat Oppression*, Lisa Schoenfielder and Barb Wieser (eds.), Rotunda Press, Glasgow, Aunt Lute Book Company, Iowa City, 1983.

5. See Annie Sprinkle's auto-biographical *Post Porn Modernist*, Torch Books, Amsterdam, 1991.

6. For an interesting discussion of the emergence of a more inclusive approach to sexuality in 'queer politics', see Cherry Smyth's contribution to the 'Lesbians Talk' series from Scarlet Press, London, in *Lesbians Talk Queer Notions*, 1992.

Recommended Reading

Assiter, Alison, *Pornography and Feminism*, Pluto Press, London, 1989.

Brownmiller, Susan, *Femininity*, Simon & Schuster, 1984; Paladin, London, 1986.

Caught Looking, *Caught Looking: Feminism, Pornography, and Censorship*, Caught Looking, Inc., New York, 1986.

Feminists Against Censorship, *Pornography & Feminism: The Case Against Censorship*, Gillian Rodgerson and Elizabeth Wilson (eds.) Lawrence & Wishart, London, 1991.

Firestone, Shulamith, *The Dialectic of Sex*, William Morrow & Company, Inc., New York, 1970.

Hawkins, Gordon and Zimring, Frankline E., *Pornography in a Free Society*, Cambridge University Press, Cambridge and New York, 1988 (paperback 1991).

Hunt, Margaret, 'The De-eroticization of Women's Liberation: Social Purity Movements and the Revolutionary Feminism of Sheila Jeffreys', *Feminist Review* no. 34, (Perverse Politics: Lesbian Issues), spring 1990.

Segal, Lynne, 'Pornography and Violence: What the "Experts" Really Say', *Feminist Review*, no. 36, autumn 1990.

Segal, Lynne and McIntosh, Mary, (eds.) *Sex Exposed: Sexuality and the Pornography Debate*, Virago, London, 1992.

Smyth, Cherry, *Lesbians Talk Queer Notions*, Scarlet Press, London, 1992.

Sprinkle, Annie, *Post Porn Modernist*, Torch Books, Amsterdam, 1991.

Thompson, W., Annetts, J., et al., *Soft-Core: A Content Analysis of Legally Available Pornography in Great Britain 1968–1990 and the Implications of Aggression Research*, Reading University, 1990.

Vance, Carole S., ed., *Pleasure and Danger*, Routledge & Kegan Paul, Boston, London, Melbourne and Henley, 1984.

Williams, Linda, *Hard Core: Power, Pleasure, and the 'Frenzy of the Visible'*, Pandora Press, London, 1990.

Index